C0-ARS-366

COMMUNITY ORGANIZATION, 1961

COMMUNITY ORGANIZATION 1961

PAPERS PRESENTED AT
THE 88TH ANNUAL FORUM OF THE
NATIONAL CONFERENCE ON SOCIAL WELFARE

PUBLISHED 1961 FOR
THE NATIONAL CONFERENCE ON SOCIAL WELFARE
by COLUMBIA UNIVERSITY PRESS, *New York and London*

Published by Columbia University Press

Library of Congress Catalog Card Number: 60-15147

Manufactured in the United States of America

FOREWORD

THE PAPERS IN THIS VOLUME were selected from among those submitted for presentation at the 88th Annual Forum in the Twin Cities on the subject of community organization under the auspices of the National Conference on Social Welfare Program Committee and by the Associate Groups. The emphasis of the program on physical, social, and health planning, experimental approaches in deprived areas, the role of community welfare planning in intergroup relations, and new studies and methods in community organization is reflected in these papers. In selecting these fifteen papers from among the fifty submitted the Selection Committee strove to cover as wide a range of subject matter as possible. They then added the paper on "The Function of Social Work" by Dr. Jan de Jongh, delivered at the Tenth International Conference of Social Work at Rome, and its discussion by Herman Stein at the Annual Forum to provide a world setting for the other community organization papers.

Two of the papers have a research approach; one, by Olmsted, on the analysis of social work jobs which was done in Cleveland and used for community planning; the other, on the broader study of the community organization process, by Morris. Two papers on the problems of youth in the community discuss the educational factors (Saltzman) and the effect of the expanding youth population on the agencies serving youth (Beck). Two papers on intergroup relationships, by Culberson and Pantoja, reflect the importance of this aspect of community planning. The relationships of public and voluntary agencies in the over-all community picture are discussed by Bachman, Schorr, and Kramer. The professional practice of the community organization specialty is outlined by Dutton and Schenk, while Anderson emphasizes the health aspects of community planning. A paper by Toll, telling of the role of the state mental hospital in the community, describes a revealing project on a specialized problem. The Hillman paper presents the community organization program as it is being applied to selected deprived areas, with its implications for other areas.

No one forum can cover all aspects of community organization, but the Committee was gratified that there were significant papers covering a wide range of interests.

The Committee which selected this volume was composed of Charles Wright, Community Health and Welfare Council of Hennepin County, and Edward Francel, School of Social Work, University of Minnesota, in addition to the chairman. They were given able staff assistance in their difficult task by Ruth M. Williams, Assistant Executive Secretary of NCSW.

THOMAS SHERRARD
Chairman, Selection Committee for Community Organization Papers

Chicago
August, 1961

CONTENTS

THE CONTRIBUTORS

GAYLORD W. ANDERSON, M.D., Mayo Professor and Director, School of Public Health, College of Medical Sciences, University of Minnesota, Minneapolis

RICHARD S. BACHMAN, Executive Director, Ohio Citizens' Council for Health and Welfare, Columbus

BERTRAM M. BECK, Associate Executive Director, National Association of Social Workers, New York

GEORGE W. CULBERSON, Executive Director, Pittsburgh Commission on Human Relations; President, National Association of Intergroup Relations Officials

J. F. DE JONGH, Director, Amsterdam School of Social Work, Amsterdam, the Netherlands

W. C. DUTTON, JR., Executive Director, American Institute of Planners, Washington, D.C.

ARTHUR HILLMAN, Director, Training Center at Hull House, National Federation of Settlements and Neighborhood Centers, Chicago

RALPH M. KRAMER, Executive Director, Contra Costa Community Welfare Council, Richmond, Calif.

ROBERT MORRIS, Associate Professor of Community Welfare Planning, Florence Heller Graduate School for Advanced

Studies in Social Welfare, Brandeis University, Waltham, Mass.

C. B. OLMSTED, Personnel Adviser, Welfare Federation, Cleveland

ANTONIA PANTOJA, Director, Community Relations Division, New York City Commission on Intergroup Relations

HENRY SALTZMAN, Program Specialist on the Great Cities, Grey Area Program, Ford Foundation, New York

QUENTIN F. SCHENK, Associate Professor of Social Work and Coordinator, Community Development Program, University of Missouri School of Social Work, Columbia

ALVIN L. SCHORR, U.S. Department of Health, Education and Welfare, Social Security Administration, Division of Program Research, Washington, D.C.

HERMAN D. STEIN, Director of Research Center, New York School of Social Work, Columbia University, New York

JOSEPH F. TOLL, School of Social Work, University of Maryland, Baltimore

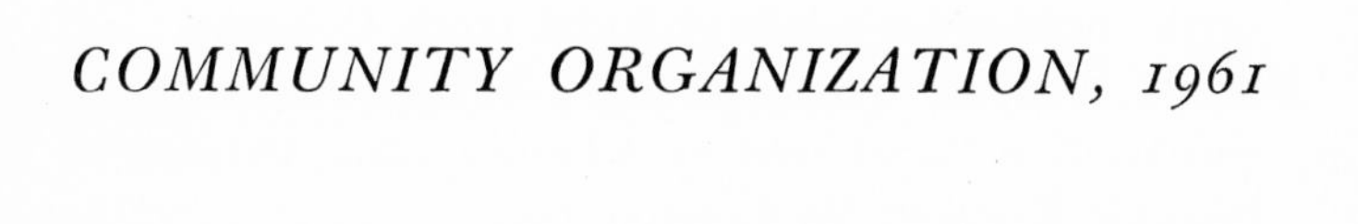

COMMUNITY ORGANIZATION, 1961

THE FUNCTION OF SOCIAL WORK

by J. F. de Jongh

THERE IS SUCH an incredible confusion of words when social workers talk with one another. Let us look particularly at the words "social work." They are used in at least four meanings:

1. Sometimes they indicate a field of action or a certain kind of activity in society, as when we talk about "the role of citizen leaders in social work" or about "social work as a primary and a secondary function."

2. Sometimes we do not mean a field of action at all but the community of agencies that are doing social work, as when we talk about the "responsibilities of social work and social workers to clients and society."

3. At other moments we use the term "social work" definitely not to indicate the agencies but the social workers themselves, as, for example, when we speak of cooperation and teamwork "between social work and other professions."

4. Finally, we sometimes use "social work" when we have in mind the body of knowledge and skills, as when we talk about "the contribution of the social sciences to social work."

In discussing the "function of social work" I shall leave aside the complexities of the concept of function, with which modern sociology has so nicely confronted us and will only say that I use the word "function" as almost synonymous with the word "task." But it is not so easy to determine what we mean by "social work." For the time being, however, let us think of social work as a certain kind of activity in society or, even better, as a group of activities which together form a field of action. This I think is the basic meaning, which makes it more understandable that sometimes the same words are used to indicate the group of agencies or of workers who perform these activities and sometimes the body of knowledge developed in connection with them.

What field of action do we have in mind when we talk about social work? It seems to me that at this point much of the confusion in our terminology and thinking originates. Sometimes we have in mind the activities of all people who try to work together or to help other people to solve social problems of various kinds or to improve the conditions of life. Sometimes, however, we mean the activities of people who have a special competence to deal with certain more or less specific human and social problems. These are, in fact, two entirely different concepts of social work. They have very different implications.

A discussion becomes entirely meaningless if the participants use the same words for different concepts without being aware of it. We should therefore try to find different words. Why should we not use the term "social welfare activities" to indicate the broad concept encompassing any activity of individuals and groups and communities to improve the quality of our social life? That would be in accordance with the concept of social welfare as it is being used in many countries. But then, why could we not limit the term "social work" to the activities around specific problems that require the competence of specialists?

Social welfare is an activity carried on by ordinary men and women, by many citizens and various kinds of agencies, all interested in, and willing to work for, the betterment of the conditions of their fellow citizens or their communities. It makes an appeal to all citizens to contribute whatever they have to give of energy, knowledge, or money. It appears in many different forms—individual help from man to man; agency programs to serve special purposes; activity of small groups or whole communities to improve community conditions; action to get social legislation or other government measures, and so on. With what kind of problems social welfare will deal, or we could also say its function, depends mainly on three factors:

1. The social reality of a country and its needs
2. The philosophy of that nation: its awareness of needs; its value system according to which it feels responsible for doing something about those needs
3. The social resources in that country, including the human resources in terms of the citizens' awareness of responsibility for each other.

Social welfare is by its very nature a vague concept because it is so broad, encompasses so much, and appears under so many forms in different countries. It may be the activity of a women's organization which brings hot meals to old people who live alone. Or the action of a group of citizens who are trying to create open places and playgrounds in their neighborhood, or of a Rotary club that collects money for fellowships. Or the efforts of a teacher to organize after-school recreation for the children. Thousands of examples could be given of activities of individuals and groups in all areas of community life. Together they form the concept of social welfare. It can hardly be further defined and circumscribed, so varying are the forms, purposes, and means.

Social work, in the more limited sense in which I shall use the term, emerges gradually from the social welfare field. In the course of his action to improve the conditions of life man continually meets obstacles. One is his lack of knowledge of what causes certain phenomena and of how to deal with them. So man is continually studying those phenomena and in doing so develops fields of special knowledge, a competence to diagnose and understand certain human needs, and to deal with them. So many professions gradually emerge out of this human activity. Public health, housing, and education, with their specialized knowledge and skills, have sprung from, or have been highly stimulated by, social welfare activities. This process is still going on, because constantly new problems are being brought under scientific observation and new knowledge and skills may spring from that observation and the related thinking and research. It seems to me that we might consider social work also as such a specialized activity, largely provoked by social welfare interests and activities.

What, then, is the specialized field of social work? Or, in other words, what is the function of social work in the limited sense of the term? I believe that I am consistent with historic reality when I state that modern social work started when some social welfare workers began to study the social breakdown of individuals and families in its many forms of chronic poverty, family disintegration, alcoholism, delinquency, prostitution, and so forth. They began to see these phenomena as indications of maladjustment between the individual—or the family—and the social surroundings. So a special insight developed into the general problem of the relationships between the individual and the surrounding groups, between the individual and the agencies, the social institution and the law. Concurrent with the growth of this insight there was the development of skills in talking with people in need, in relating to them, in influencing their thinking, feeling, and behavior, in using agency resources to help them. This activity of dealing with social problems cases in a more scientific way has been—and still is, in many countries—the core of social work activity, the main function for which social workers have been trained. It is a specialized service within the social welfare equipment of society.

So far, the relationship between social welfare activities and social work probably is comparatively simple. But many of us will not be satisfied by this description of the function of social work. That is understandable because actually, starting from their special knowledge about individual social problems and dissatisfied with the purely individualized methods to deal with those problems, some social workers moved on to study the community surroundings of their clients and the ways to influence those surroundings more directly. They were not the only ones interested in community problems. From several other sides, practical as well as scientific—city planners, public health workers, sociologists, social psychologists—the same interest in the meaning and problems of communities developed. And so there emerged a new specialty in the social welfare field, to deal with problems of communities as such. This specialty studies phenomena such as community tensions, community apathy, community impotence, even community breakdown and the ways to influence the development and activity of a community. Here too, though as yet far less than in the field of social problems of individuals, a body of specialized knowledge and skills is growing rapidly. We usually find it listed under "community development" or "community organization."

Now there is some controversy on this subject. Some think that dealing with social problems of individuals and dealing with community problems require the same attitudes, knowledge, and skills to such an extent that it is justified to bring both together under "social work." Others, however, are inclined to consider that contending with community problems requires somewhat different equipment and is a new and separate profession. Personally, I sympathize with the first opinion. The fact that the body of knowledge in the field of community organization has largely been evolved at schools of social work strengthens my point of view.

Whether we confine social work to dealing with social problems or whether we include community problems, social work in this conception is by definition an activity of professional people trained in a scientific approach to certain social problems. The function of social work is delineated by its actual competence. Social workers can only claim a function as such in so far as they have professional competence. This professional competence varies from country to country. In some countries it has as yet been developed hardly at all, either because the facilities are lacking or because its importance, the contribution which it can make to the social welfare field, has not yet been recognized. In other countries, the emphasis in the training of social workers has been for a long time entirely on acquiring competence to deal with certain social problems of individuals. There are also countries in which the schools may try to inculcate competence in working with community problems. So, there are in the social work field, just as in the social welfare field, considerable differences between countries. Yet, in so far as there are basic skills in dealing with human beings and human communities, the training institutions in different countries may easily learn from each other. That explains why it is possible to have an international body of scientific social work knowledge and skills and why social workers may communicate with each other somewhat more easily than do social welfare workers.

I hope it has become clear that in using the words "social welfare activities" and "social work" in such a way we get two different concepts, each of which corresponds to a social reality with its own character and its own importance. Both should be conceived of dynamically: there is nothing static there. Social welfare activities may grow and change as the needs of the countries change, the awareness of needs deepens, the resources increase. Social work may grow and change as its competence develops, as it brings new problems within its orbit. Both social work and social welfare, therefore, are activities whose actual functions are continually changing, though through different causes.

This distinction between social welfare activities and social work has a number of implications. By definition there are implications so far as training is concerned. Social work is an activity of trained specialists who are usually professionals. Social welfare is the field of laymen who feel their responsibility as citizens.

There are implications for leadership. There can be no doubt that leadership in the social welfare field really belongs to the community and to citizen leaders. Social welfare activities are based on choices which the citizens and the community make. Even if, in the process, other people have to be appointed to carry out the work, the responsibility, for the main direction of the activities still remains with those who have initiated them.

In social work, the situation is much more complicated. As soon as an activity has been developed scientifically to the point that it requires special competence, the actual supervision of the professionals can only be given by people with superior competence. That creates a delicate problem. The same problem exists in medicine. The medical profession has sometimes tried to solve it by creating a closed "medical city," excluding all lay interference and claiming almost absolute autonomy within the community. No community can accept that—as the fights in some countries about socialized medicine or the role of doctors in social security demonstrate. Nor can the community accept an autonomy of the social work profession. The community will have to decide to what extent it wants social work as a professional activity, in what fields it wants it, what the status of social workers will be, and what resources can be put at their disposal. To be able to do that, the community will have to know what the contribution of social workers to the solution of certain problems can be; in other words, the community will have to know the professional competence of social workers. But how can it, since this professional competence is based on scientific assumptions and methods of work which, more or less by definition, cannot really be judged by laymen?

Here we have a curious contradiction for which there is no basic solution. The problem of communication between the professions and the community is, of course, universal. In the case of social work, however, it is even more acute, because social work has not yet acquired the prestige which makes society accept in good faith some of the demands of the older professions. So social work will have to accept its dependence on the deepening insight of the community and on the over-all community controls. It will have to work on the basis of a compromise, consisting of a continuous effort on its part to translate what it does into simple words and to demonstrate what it actually can do. Social work cannot accept that its actual operations be supervised either by people from other professions or by nonprofessionals. Where such a situation exists, there must be either stagnation or strong frustrating tensions, because a professional will only be able to work and grow under the leadership of superior professional competence.

The distinction between social welfare activities and social work has implications also for use of volunteers, about which there are in many places the most conflicting feelings and opinions. Let me just say that it seems that in social welfare activities the volunteer is the real agent in the process, the fully qualified participant in the planning, organization, and implementation. He may rise to a leadership position and then supervise even the workers for whom social welfare has become an occupation.

In social work the situation is different. In some cases it has become exclusively the province of professionals. In some other social work processes, however, while it is not impossible to use volunteers, they usually must have a well-defined and limited task and work under the supervision of the professionals, who retain the final responsibility.

So far, the distinction which I made and the implications I have drawn may seem more or less theoretical. I am quite aware that it is not always easy really to make the distinction between social welfare activities and social work. That is partly due to the rapid development of social work knowledge and the continuously moving border lines of social work competence. Problems about which nothing really was known twenty years ago have since been studied so much that practically only a professional can now deal with them competently. But there is another factor, which sometimes makes it difficult to distinguish between social welfare activities and social work: we often find both activities in the same agency.

In general, we can say that social work competence developed gradually out of the needs of the social welfare field, because individuals and agencies were baffled by some human and social problems which they encountered and began to study them, often drawing in people from the universities and from various scientific disciplines. So it is only natural that there are in many countries many agencies which undertake the oddest combination of tasks, ranging from the most simple humanitarian activities—visiting the old, organizing New Year or Independence Day parties, and so forth—to the most difficult family casework assignments or group work with street gangs. Of course, there are everywhere still agencies, women's organizations, or service clubs which take on only social welfare activities. And there are agencies organized only to do specific social work jobs. But it is the social welfare agencies which begin to employ social workers, or agencies in other professional fields which begin to reach out into the social field, which present problems.

There are problems of how to distribute the tasks. When the social worker enters such an agency there is a tendency to lay upon his shoulders responsibility for all the activities of the agency, regardless of whether they fall within the sphere of his professional competence or not. That can be frustrating for the social worker, and it certainly is not an efficient use of the limited number of professionals in our field.

There are also problems of leadership. The social worker is not competent to carry on all social welfare activities, and the responsibility for them should remain with the lay leaders of the agencies. On the other hand, within his own sphere of competence the social worker should be his own master unless superior professional supervision is available in the agency.

I venture to suggest that the use of this distinction between social welfare activities and social work will help to clarify some of the problems in our agencies: problems of personnel and leadership; problems of choice of function and distribution of tasks; problems in the use of volunteers, and so on. It will at least help us to realize that not all our agencies perform functions of the same character, and that alone may help us to perform both functions better.

Let us again turn to the question of the essence of the social work function. I described social work as a complex of specialized services, mostly growing out of the social welfare field as specialized knowledge and professional competence develop in dealing with individual social problems and in dealing with community problems. So far as individual social work is concerned, I think the description is right: it really is a specialized service with its own field, comparable to the medical services, the educational services, and so on. Its emergence is caused by the growing intricacies of our social structure, by the changing cultural patterns, and by our increasing awareness of the needs of millions of individual human beings who are bewildered under the impact of these social forces. I am afraid that we shall need individual social work more and more in the world to come, and therefore we must hope that it will continue to deepen and widen the special body of knowledge and skills on which its competence to deal with the social problems of the individual is based.

What about community organization? It too is certainly developing and using a specialized body of knowledge and skills. What is the place of the community organization function within the social welfare field? Is it, again just like individual social work, a specialized field, another compartment of social welfare? Or is it more than that? Can it be more? Should it be more? Is it possible that the science and skill of community organization might lead us to consider it not as a specialized compartment, but as a method of work which has relevance for all social welfare action?

Please allow me a few remarks at this point which may seem to be a digression. I submitted to you a definition of social welfare activities, emphasizing that they were essentially activities of citizens as such, not based on any specialized competence. But is it not natural to expect that these social welfare activities will also, as such, become more and more the object of scientific research? To what extent will a science of social welfare problems and a scientific skill to deal with them develop?

Some of you will remember that in the summer of 1959 the United Nations Economic and Social Council discussed a report, prepared by what was called at that time a committee of five wise men under the chairmanship of our distinguished President George Davidson, and dealing with the future activities in the social and economic field of the UN and the specialized agencies.[1] This report provoked a

[1] Five Year Perspective 1960–1964 (United Nations Publications No. 60 IV. 14).

comment from the Secretary General of the UN.[2] The two documents together still make the most fascinating reading. There we do see the emergence of the concept of a social welfare policy as a whole. For a century or longer we have been looking at social welfare problems more or less fragmentarily: we dealt separately with health problems, or housing problems, or education or delinquency, or many other forms of individual maladjustment. And we are still largely doing that. But we did become aware of some of the interrelationships between the various fields. The development problems of the underdeveloped countries as well as the tremendous technological changes in the already industrialized areas of the world are bringing home to us, often in the hard way, that all social problems are interrelated, as they are also related with economic development and with changing cultural values. We are studying the character of these relationships—the UN biennial reports on the world social situation are making a great contribution in this respect. We shall also have to study and learn the methods to deal with the various fields in a more integrated way, but at least we are aware of the need for such a new approach, which would really bring us a new social welfare policy.

Now let us return to the questions about community organization. Is community organization related to the emerging concept of an integrated social welfare policy? In some ways, yes. A community organizer usually works with a small community; but he has to look at it as a whole, he has to help his community to think about the various aspects of social welfare and their interrelationships, to discover the over-all resources of the community and to de-

[2] Programme Appraisal 1959–1964; note of the Secretary General (United Nations document E/3260/Rev. 1).

termine priorities. He therefore needs certain knowledge and skills which can be transferred to the problems of the wider community. Community organization, therefore, starting from its limited field, can and should contribute to the framing of a social welfare policy.

But does that mean that the community organizers will become the social welfare workers par excellence, that they will have to move into a leadership function in the social welfare field? Then the relationship between social welfare activities and social work, as I described it, would be fundamentally reversed. I put the question this way because there are tendencies in that direction. The community and the agencies sometimes try to put upon the social worker the whole responsibility for social welfare, and the social workers themselves sometimes claim a leadership function in the whole social welfare field. I continue to think that that is wrong, even if the community organizer can make a great contribution to the social welfare field. His contribution, however, can only be a technical one: a contribution of methods to study the community and the interrelationships between various needs and actions; a contribution also of methods to help the community to determine needs and resources and to decide upon aims and policy. But those decisions, the decisions on priorities and aims and policies, should remain the decisions of the community itself, of the citizens. In these matters of social policy just as in politics, it should not be a small group of professional technicians which frames the life of the community, but the community itself. The community organizer, when functioning in the social welfare field as a whole, will basically be a public servant, a public servant who has a professional service to offer but who remains a servant. May I quote from those memorable words which the Secretary General of the United Nations, Mr. Dag Hammarskjold, spoke when he took up his duties in New York in April, 1953:

> The public servant is there in order to assist, so to say from the inside, those who take the decisions which frame history. He should—as I see it—listen, analyze, and learn to understand fully the forces at work and the interests at stake, so that he will be able to give the right advice when the situation calls for it. Don't think that he—in following this line of personal policy—takes but a passive part in the development. It is a most active one. But he is active as an instrument, a catalyst, perhaps an inspirer—he serves.[3]

So it seems that, indeed, individual social work and community organization can both be conceived of as specialized services even if we consider them both as social work functions. Yet they are very different: individual social work is more a section that deals with special problems of individuals, whereas community organization might rather be considered a method by which to achieve social welfare aims.

Now that we have looked into the function of social welfare and the function of social work within the social welfare field, let us consider social work in relation to, and working with, other groups and disciplines. Why is the collaboration of social workers with other professional groups so often really something of a problem? Why, as soon as social workers meet other professional people, is there often a certain tension, a tension which may even build up to a complete incapacity to understand each other and work together?

I think that here, too, part of the phenomenon can be ascribed to a lack of clarity about our function and that a clearer terminology will be helpful. For, if we, both social

[3] *United Nations Bulletin,* April 15, 1953 p. 266.

work agencies and social workers, in our contacts with other professional people, describe our own role in the broad and vague terms which we use so often, and which practically amount to the concept of social welfare as I have used it here, it is inevitable that we antagonize almost everybody else. We seem, then, to claim a monopoly on an activity in which many more people and many other professions are as interested as we are. We seem, moreover, to claim leadership in a field, parts of which at least can also be claimed—and it may be with more right—by other professions: social hygiene, by the medical profession; recreation, by teachers; community relations, by local government staff; marriage guidance, by the clergy; and so on. Social welfare has so many aspects that many groups and professions have a stake in it.

We should begin by recognizing that in the social welfare field social workers perform only a specialized and therefore a limited function. But that is only part of the problem, for even that limited role is often questioned and challenged, and particularly by other helping professions. From that challenge spring some of our most bitter clashes with the medical profession, with the teachers, with the clergy. To understand these clashes better we have to realize first of all that as social workers we are moving in an almost entirely new area. Consideration of intrapsychic reactions to the outer factors of life and to other human beings, and therefore of human relationships, has only recently become subject to scientific exploration and conscious action. Social work as such is part of this scientific development. It grew out of the preoccupation of philanthropists and social scientists with the phenomena of social maladjustment and human breakdown. For these pioneer social workers the problems of human relationships seemed to be the most natural field of study and action, and so they began to consider themselves as specialists in this new vocation—and sometimes by right.

It so happened, however, that these early social workers were not the only ones to be interested. The medical profession, starting from its preoccupation with bodily and mental diseases, rediscovered the relationship with the social environment, ventured into the unknown with its research, and tried to extend the borders of its practical activity. So did the clergy, when they began to realize again to what extent individual human relationships and community tensions influenced not only the behavior but also the feelings and basic thinking of their flock. And so, here and there, did the teachers, who cared for the children and found that their ability to learn was greatly hampered by their social needs. We could go on giving examples of how various professions, each on the basis of its own originally limited purpose, have been reaching out to this new field of human adjustment and human relationships. This has really become a common ground of many professions. Each entered the area at the corner nearest his own original field. I think Seward Hiltner, by using the metaphor of the village green and elaborating upon it, has made some of the most illuminating remarks ever given on this subject.[4]

It is quite clear, therefore, that it is the scientific development itself, the rediscovery of the oneness of the human being, the rediscovery of the interrelatedness of physical, mental, and social factors, which motivate the helping professions to transcend their original borders and to widen

[4] Seward Hiltner, "Tension and Mutual Support among the Helping Professions," *Social Service Review,* XXXI (1957), 377–89.

their functions. And then they clash with other professions which do the same. And often they all clash with social work, for which human relationship is the natural field!

So the scientific development has not only created our function as social workers, it has also changed the function of other professions and it certainly is one of the causes of the tension between the helping professions. But it certainly is not the only one. Sometimes it seems as if there is an even more basic animosity between the helping professions. And I think there really is. Social workers, used to introspection, might be aware of it more easily than others. The animosity is often hidden, but when it is visible we see that it really is deeply rooted in human nature, with a kind of love at its base, but a possessive love. Each helping profession which has a strong interest in human beings has also a tendency toward a "totalitarian" relationship and therefore resents the intrusion of other helpers. Unfortunately, possessive love seems to be the most normal kind of love, and professional people in the helping professions continue to be normal people for whom a totalitarian helping relationship seems to be more satisfying than the giving of help in a limited context.

The trouble is also that this basic tendency toward a totalitarian relationship gets a new stimulus from the emphasis on the oneness of the human being and the interrelatedness of all the aspects of his life. So, the scientific development seems to provide a new and wonderful justification for the totalitarian demands of all the helping professions. The doctors want to deal with the whole human being—and so do the nurses—and the teachers—and the priests—and the social workers.

I question whether it is possible at all to deal with the

human being as a whole, in view of the innumerable aspects of, and forces in, a human being. I also question whether we have the right, when somebody asks for help in a certain problem of his life, to impose ourselves upon him in that totalitarian way.

There is another aspect of the problem. Let us remember that the scientific development which has brought to light the interrelatedness of the various elements of human life should also make us aware of our limitations in dealing with them. The right of the professions to deal with human beings cannot be based on intentions or on general vague notions, but only on intimate knowledge and experienced skill. Now if there is one thing which modern scientific development brings home to us, it is this that each of us can hope to have this intimate knowledge and skill in a limited field only. The maximum we can hope for is a certain awareness of the complexity of the whole and of the importance of many factors. That awareness we all urgently need, but it will only underline the limitations of our own competence. That applies to all the helping professions. That should also mean that each of us should be happy when other professions explore part of the unknown field. It may increase the knowledge available about human problems as well as the equipment to deal with them.

The problem is not that there is common ground and the problem is not that we meet each other there. A problem arises only when each profession thinks that it can claim this ground as exclusively its own. Then they are working against the real human interests. The professions should claim a function only in so far as their professional competence goes. That is by definition true for social work, but it should also be true for other professions, whose potential scope can be circumscribed more easily. It is easy to claim a field; it is less easy to build up enough competence to justify the claim. We are sometimes inclined to base our claims not on the actual qualification of the average social worker but on the outstanding performances of some of our most able colleagues—and it is natural that other professions with more mature and more standardized professional skills do not easily accept these claims based on future skills. But other professions also base their claims on possible future competence when, because of a scientific recognition of interrelationships, they want to extend their function into the social field. Once more let us recognize that, for each of us, function can only be based on competence. Love and devotion are essential for all professions, but they are not a justification for going beyond one's capability. That does not solve all the problems of cooperation between the professions, but it is an extremely good starting point. It gives us a basic modesty and the willingness to see the others as colleagues who are exploring the same unknown field. It also implies that there will be no fixed and no fixable border lines. But does that matter? There is work enough for all of us, and we shall need each other constantly. Unfortunately, modern society and the changes therein make life so difficult, so complicated, for millions of human beings that there is more work than we can ever hope to accomplish, much less accomplish alone.

These reflections on the function of social work have led to a distinction between two functions: social welfare and social work. Both have a tremendous and fascinating role to play. Both find their limits in the human beings which have to perform them, and it is wisdom to recognize those limitations. But that can never be our last word, because our actual limitations are not our ultimate frontiers. For social welfare there will always be the unmet needs of the nations, which require more devotion and more inspired action. For social work there will always be unexplored human problems, which require exploration. So our very functions will require us to move on and forward, together with the other helping professions, in one common battle against human need and human ignorance.

DISCUSSION

by Herman D. Stein

THE MAJOR DISTINCTION that Dr. de Jongh makes between social work and social welfare is recognized in the United States,[1] if only implicitly. Social welfare is generally seen as encompassing the larger social needs and resources of the nation, and social work is seen as one of the professions within social welfare. There is a basic unrest, however, about this relationship within American social work, with the conviction in many quarters that we should as a profession have more direct influence on the development of social welfare policy and not through community organization alone. The gap between social work and social welfare policy is seen in terms of professional motivation, competence, and access to social welfare policy.

There has been a shift in professional motivation from social work's preoccupation with the individual—not com-

[1] Mr. Stein was asked to discuss Dr. de Jongh's paper with particular relevance to social work in the United States.

plete, but quite distinct. The evidence in activity within the National Association of Social Workers alone in developing over the years what amounts to a social welfare platform, for example, attests to the changing climate. By "competence" I refer to the need seen for specialized training to evaluate social welfare policy and to formulate such policy—not as the exclusive province of the community organizer, but also of administrators in their professional roles, and of all social workers through participation in agency policy and through professional associations and other groups which can take positions on social welfare questions. By "access to social welfare policy" I refer to the availability of employment in welfare policy positions for social workers and the availability to the profession of leverage and influence in broad welfare concerns. There is discomfort in American social work as to all three: the extent of the motivation; the extent of the competence we have gained; and the opportunity or access for influence and work in social welfare concerns.

Citizen control over social welfare decisions is indeed important, but I have some question about Dr. de Jongh's formulation in the sense that the citizen leans heavily on technical specialists to supply, if not the direction, at least clarity as to alternatives and their consequences. And once decisions are made, the social worker participates as an expert in carrying out plans. The demarcation between social welfare and social work may not be so clear-cut as Dr. de Jongh suggests. Urban redevelopment is a case in point. What happens to the dislocated residents of a neighborhood whose buildings are leveled to the ground? City planners, architects, builders, public health officials, are all involved. Urban redevelopment is clearly in the area of social welfare.

But until recently social workers—and only in a handful of situations now—have not been involved in policy at any level, nor in staff positions related to urban redevelopment. Social workers have something to contribute to the making of the very decisions that now concern other professions, occupations, and political groups.

Juvenile delinquency provides another illustration. There is increasing unrest with limiting the professional habitat of social workers who deal with juvenile delinquency to clinics where delinquency is treated as an emotional problem of the individual, or to treatment-centered institutions for the juvenile offender, or to probation and parole systems. Much more interest is being aroused in the whole pattern of social etiology in delinquency, the elements that give rise to and buttress this form of social deviance, that make it difficult to reinforce socially conforming behavior or permit the offender who leaves the institution "rehabilitated" to stay that way. How social workers can become professionally involved in affecting this social etiology is, however, far from clear.

It is not that social work is attempting in this instance, or should attempt, to do all the things that are needed to mediate between the individual and the social setting. Rather, with the help of other professions and nonprofessional groups, the central notion is to find a way to help change the very social conditions which give rise to or sustain delinquent patterns, as well as to provide therapeutic intervention on an individual or group basis where needed.

In other words, the movement in this country is in the direction of getting closer to social welfare problems from a professional base; not usurping the activity of other professions but finding our specific contribution. The useful distinctions between social work and social welfare which Dr. de Jongh emphasizes become then a statement of relationship, not simply of difference.

There is more than a definitional question involved. It is essentially a matter of social values. How are the energies of social workers to be used? What disposition of scant professional resources should be made? If the profession's contribution is seen in terms of enhancing professional expertise in its service, social work energies will tend to go into the refinement and elaboration of techniques. If social *welfare* objectives are seen as paramount, energies will be directed toward participation with other professions and lay groups, with a professional base that can become more amorphous.

The pendulum is swinging in this country toward greater social welfare concern because of the sense of imbalance that has developed in the profession. Social work education is participating in this redirection. The emphasis on the social environment, through relating the social sciences to social work practice, is gradually compelling more sophisticated attention to the social context in which human problems arise, to their social as well as individual and familial etiology and treatment possibilities. Practitioners who deal with the individual are hopefully working with him increasingly in relation to his social milieu, more cognizant of the strains within the social system which give rise to the behavior, more aware of the social and cultural aspects of human behavior. To the extent that social agencies have concern about social welfare issues and provide access to participation by the professionals within them, caseworkers and group workers will increasingly be able to participate in the development of social welfare objectives.

As for community organization, close as it is to social welfare in Dr. de Jongh's terms, it is still struggling to come into its own and has not entirely resolved its direction. Increasingly, it sees the terrain for its activity as larger than that of chests and councils and is moving into neighborhoods, public health and community mental health programs, and other areas that until recently were new to direct social work involvement. In many quarters distinctions between group workers and community organizers are fading. Moreover, the recommendations of the Council on Social Work Education Curriculum Committee, which approves a two-year sequence of specialization in community organization as well as the more traditional one-year major after a year in casework or group work practice, indicate that community organization is becoming more aware of its own content and method. Part of the emphasis in community organization is on participation in the formation of social welfare policy. Indeed, a fourth major method has been proposed by Dr. Eveline Burns, who suggests that social welfare policy should become a special area of professional competence, and this proposal has now itself become an issue within social work education.

This is not to say that we have arrived at an acceptable balance between social work and social welfare, or that there is room for self-congratulation in American social work. The trends are only trends, they have not been realized, but they are in the direction of developing stronger links with social welfare, moving away from a well-developed but still relatively provincial professional base.

Nor is this to suggest that the pattern of our current movement is one that necessarily fits all other nations. In many countries social work is still embedded in a broad social welfare conception without a professional base, and the need may be to acquire specialized competence and redress the balance the other way. What is important to all of social work internationally is to view the relationship as one in which social work occupies a definitive professional place among the helping professions with defined competence in relation to social needs, but tied in with larger social welfare purposes and objectives.

Dr. de Jongh has raised two points with regard to community organization which bear further comment. One is whether it belongs in social work since it is so interconnected with social welfare; the other is whether the community organizer becomes a leader or an expert. Dr. de Jongh prefers to see community organization within social work as another kind of social work. The trend in the United States is definitely in this direction, but there has also been an undercurrent, however small, which would quite radically differentiate community organization from direct individual and group service to the point where community organization would require an entirely different preparation. The logical outcome of such differentiation would put part of social work in the clinical professions and part in the community planning and public service professions. There are no signs that this is likely to occur within the foreseeable future in American social work. Individual, group, and community processes are seen as basic to social work, with different kinds of professional expertise, to be sure, but with common views of human personality, of the nature of resistance, of motivation for change, as well as common knowledge as to needs and resources and, particularly, a common core of values. These processes, it is reasonable to suggest, have come to be considered fundamental to the social work profession the world over. The investment in one or the other will differ with different needs and programs, and the extent to which they will be specialized will also vary. The community development worker, for example, is often working with all three processes, with the emphasis on community involvement rather than on individual service, but with the understanding of the individual relationship remaining essential. The family worker is usually concerned with an individual, but increasingly he finds himself involved also in group process and, at times, in community process.

The more troublesome question arises when the community organizer is viewed, as Dr. de Jongh seems to view him, essentially as a technician, as an enabler, moving at the behest of the community as a "public servant." This has indeed been the traditional view, but it is under severe reexamination. The rub comes when the social worker perceives the direction of a community program as being, in his mind, quite wrong and inimical to the best interests of the community. Does he have the right or the responsibility to voice this position in an attempt to influence community direction? Can the professional enabler really move effectively, in any case, without in some way influencing the direction of activity, if only in sharpening the alternatives or adding alternatives to be considered?

He often has to influence decision-makers if he is to be effective at all. The "enabler" technician model with a primary concern for process can become a too convenient façade behind which one absolves oneself from social responsibility. The community organizer who takes over responsibility as a citizen leader, on the other hand, is at the opposite end of the spectrum. Once this is done and the social worker is out in front he would find it hard to return to the role of professional, for he has become the representative of a cause rather than the instrument of community change through others.

In referring to the community organizer, we are of course addressing the function of the profession. It is not the function of social work either to take over lay responsibility or to be eternally neutral. It may be fair to say that community organization—indeed, social work as a whole—has not found its way out of this dilemma, but we should be less than constructive or candid if we did not concede the dilemma that lies in balancing the investment between processes and objectives, between means and ends. That democratic, ethical means are essential goes without saying. But no development which makes of social work a system of means—however sophisticated, scientific, and democratic—can satisfy us, any more than seeing social work as so preoccupied with general humanitarian social welfare goals that all claim to professional competence vanishes. Whatever else social work includes within its function, it does include values and goals as well as scientific method in helping processes, and a base in social philosophy as well as in psychology, human biology, and social sciences.

With respect to the relationship of social work to the other helping professions, there is little to add to Dr. de Jongh's discerning comments. I can only thoroughly agree that we can claim no monopoly on such concern with human welfare, that the professions will indeed continue to elbow each other, and that our position should be that the more effective work there is—from any professional base—the better. If the agricultural extension agent has social work vocabulary and techniques—well, from his point of view the social workers are using agricultural extension concepts, and what's wrong either way? Let us learn from one another, and if we indulge in interprofessional conflict, let it be conflict as to alternative ways of doing the best job, rather than fretting about whose professional terrain is being stepped on. There is ample room for all, and our energy should be directed to finding out what now lies or should lie within our capacity to contribute to society and to prepare ourselves accordingly.

Thus far we have been discussing the function of social work as if the profession itself could not only define its function but control it. This would be a fallacy. Our own understanding and convictions about our function are essential to our being able to develop it, but these are not enough. There are potent conditioning influences on the realization of the function of the social work profession, and these are not imposed solely by pressures outside social work. One vital source of influence, and often of constraint, lies in the fact that social work is an agency-based profession, using the term "agency" broadly to include all organizations that set policies and employ social workers. It is not an entrepreneurial profession; the model professional is still one who works within an organization and within its policies, even if he is operating alone in a rural area without an office or a secretary.

It is organizations, not the "profession" alone, which mediate social work functions within the social system. To the extent that the function of social work is carried out in practice today, it is through organizations and their programs. If the function of social work is to change, grow, or simply become clearer, this development must be reflected in organizational change or organizational innovation.

Why do organizations help shape the manifestations of function? Because statements of professional function are ideal; and what is actual is limited by a variety of pressures. Organizations, including those in social work, strive to survive and to accommodate to other organizations and outside influences; they have problems of control and management, and the development of allegiance by personnel to the organization, and often the major power within such organizations, lies not with professionals at all. The patterns of survival and accommodation serve to make organizational change relatively slow and not necessarily entirely in keeping with professional definitions of function.

Organizational forms set the guide lines within which the function of social work is to be expressed, and this very fact can lead to a circular definition whereby social work function is then perceived as what agencies do. Development or growth in the interpretation of professional function, moreover, does not necessarily give rise to its organizational equivalent. If we say that social work should move closer to social welfare policy, for example, this can only be done through organizations which will permit or demand that social workers do so.

It is, of course, true that the function of social work can be regarded in many different ways because "social work" itself has no single definition, and every writer on social work is at pains to define his own use of the term. But it is essential that we realize the interdependence of social work as a profession with the organizational forms within which social work is practiced. We should, and will be, perennially engaged in debating and sharpening the concept of our function. Ideally, this fundamental inquiry about the function of a profession should be addressed without reference to existing organizations, or even existing programs; otherwise, our capacity to consider the issues is restricted and befogged. The organizational framework—in whatever country—represents the practical, pragmatic actuality, and the central purpose of inquiring into professional function is to bring that actuality more into line with optimal function, and not vice versa. Otherwise, we would wind up by asking the question: "What is it that people who call themselves social workers, in agencies which are called social work agencies, say they are doing?" This is useful to know, but hardly represents a way of evolving and clarifying one's societal function.

The organizational context in which social work is carried out is not, of course, the only conditioning influence on its function. The impact of related professions and the functions they have delineated for themselves have already been alluded to. There is also the force of society's pressure. The demands of society may expand the function of social work beyond what the profession claims for itself, or may confine its function to much more restricted limits. Social work may be prodded into participating in planning the judicial and educational systems in a newly emerging nation, but may not be able to participate in personnel counseling as part of its function in an economically developed country, such as ours.

The effort to assess the function of social work is going on here, as elsewhere, in many diverse ways, even though the task is not always specified as such (for example, in the Commission on Practice of the National Association of Social Workers). But, an ongoing total look at the profession's distinctive function within social welfare has not been consistently part of our tradition, and it should be.

One approach to such an appraisal is to select certain fundamentals in a concept of a profession's function and to utilize these as a guide for examining the specifics of social work agencies, programs, and practice. The underlying purpose of all social welfare professions may be viewed as that of assisting man to develop his highest individual and collective potentialities and aspirations and to help to prevent and remedy human distress. Against this very general kind of value statement, each profession might examine its particular function by considering how the following criteria apply to it:

1. Its defined area of human need to be served
2. Its special skills and competence
3. Its relationship to social change
4. Its relationship to social control

Every profession acts on certain assumptions, explicit or implicit, congruent, confused, or conflicting, with regard to each of these criteria. An appraisal of the actual status of each in a given country could help to reveal the underlying function of the profession being examined, as it operates in that society.

The area of human need to be served represents one of the most perplexing of these criteria for social work. Economic dependency and child neglect have been the traditional starting points for social work, but the scope of human needs to which social work is addressed in this country has ramified year after year. Marital distress and lack of neighborhood leadership, rehabilitation of the chronically ill and adjustment problems of men in the armed forces, delinquency and aging and alcoholism and mental illness—what is the unifying theme of all these and many more? Is social work concerned with all human needs that involve interpersonal relationships? Then why does our professional function not include direct service in the attack on prejudice and discrimination? Is it that we should help individuals or groups to make better use of their capacities in relation to their social environment? Then why exclude the needs of workers in their industrial setting? Are inconsistencies simply the result of happenstance or do they truly reflect the priorities of human need to which professional resources should be directed, in the light of social work function?

Such questions imply not criticism, but the kinds of lines of inquiry which might compel us to clarify the breadth and also the limits of our function with respect to the dimensions of human need. A view of the perception of human needs to be met that is implicit in the way social work operates around the globe reveals great variety—from a conception of social work as largely concerned with hunger and disease to the conception that it is focused on the adjustment of problems of individuals—and I have no intention of derogating the importance of the latter. This range of conception stems from the same concern for human welfare, yet the emphasis on function can be radically different.

It is neither essential nor possible that the definitions or priorities of function be identical everywhere, but we should recognize the diversity as well as the common elements. The question "What are you trying to help with?" has to be faced within each country, if clarity is to be achieved about any profession's current or changing function within the gamut of social welfare. Moreover, to recognize the extent both of congruence and of dissimilarity of human needs to which social work is addressed, would help us see the extent to which we truly do have a central function cutting across national lines and diverse social and cultural systems. There are common human needs, but this does not necessarily mean that social work is everywhere dealing with the same definitions.

As to skills and competence, every profession must have a set considered unique, if it is to claim its rights and responsibilities as a profession, and have these accepted by society. Despite recurrent dissatisfaction with our kit of skills, social work has them—more developed in certain methods than in others, perhaps, but special skills nonetheless. The extent to which the area of competence is accepted by society as well as by related professions, however, has some bearing on the actual function permitted to social work. Moreover, constant scrutiny of the relation of these skills is necessary if we are to meet the human needs perceived to lie within the profession's province.

Social change and social control are two sides of the same coin, but they should be approached separately.

The relationship of a profession to social change involves such questions as its commitment to specific causes that necessarily involve change; for example, the reduction of illiteracy, the expansion of production, improvement in child-rearing practices, reduction of infant mortality, and so on. These "causes," to refer back to Porter R. Lee's historic use of the term, may lie within stated national policy, or primarily within the value system of the profession. The change conception also involves the extent of the profession's commitment to engage in promoting change processes, without predetermined objectives other than setting change in motion. The assumption is that the process will lead to some benefit; for example, in the development of neighborhood organization which can lead to a variety of end results. The key question here is: How much of the profession's resources—what part of its function—is to be devoted to social change goals and processes as a commitment?

By "social control," we refer generally to the profession's stake in promoting stability and integration. The "social defense" area of activity in the United Nations is essentially concerned with control. So are the "adjustment" emphasis, the prevention of family breakup, and virtually all institutional programs. Social welfare professions are all occupied to varying degrees with social control. In assessing the function of a profession in social welfare, it can be both useful and illuminating to consider the actual and optimum balance between its emphasis on social change and on social control.

Against the background of an analysis of these kinds of criteria, one may view the pattern of social work organizations and programs and the system of professional education. These are essentially derivative, emanating from basic premises as to the profession's societal function.

No definition with regard to any of these criteria need be static, but at any one time an assessment should be present with regard to each; not simply from the point of view of ideology, but based also on reality. It would be well for professional bodies in each country to evolve their concepts in these or similar terms and to consider, however tentatively, the pattern of the actual against the professional function thus defined.

If an exchange of such a country-by-country experience in analysis—whether philosophical or empirical—could take place under continuing international auspices, it would provide a vital channel for greater clarity and, what is more important, for greater service by our profession. Whatever may be our problems in clarifying our multisided function, we do have one—and whatever else may be said about social work, as a world-wide profession it includes being not only a servant of mankind but a watchdog over its essential welfare and human values. The effort at clarification is to enrich our capacities for helping, not to pin insignia on ourselves. This is a premise which is shared by Dr. de Jongh in his stimulating contribution to our thinking about the function of the social work profession.

INTERCOMMUNITY RESEARCH

by Robert Morris

SOCIAL WORK RESEARCH at the community level is entering a new era. Its past has been characterized by the local study or survey, a method concentrating upon the rich uniqueness of each community. Planning today requires knowledge not readily yielded by this approach, for professional staffs seek common principles and methods which can be applied in more than one community. Even more urgently needed is knowledge about those conditions which lead to success or failure in planning.

The method of comparative intercommunity analysis is one which permits simultaneous study of action in several communities. It holds out the promise of uncovering new knowledge about basic factors in planning. As a research method, it extends the range of inquiry which began with the individual client, moved to small groups of individuals, and then to a study of agencies as formal social institutions functioning in the community. We are now at the point of treating the entire community as a unit for study, which requires access to several similar units in order to yield the advantages of comparative analysis.

This approach, while relatively new for social work, has been attempted by other disciplines, especially anthropology and sociology. Several examples have value for social work thinking: the analysis of values in two communities by Vogt and O'Dea; [1] Angell's method for ranking community welfare effort; [2] and Miller's study of community decision-making.[3]

I believe the time has been reached when we must ask ourselves: Does social work offer the means to study its own programs and practices in similar fashion? Can we study numbers of community actions in a search for similarities and differences and thus slowly unravel in more precise fashion the central characteristics of social change under varying conditions?

Certain general conclusions may be derived from two reasonably large-scale intercommunity studies in which the author participated. The first study, carried on in the early 1950s in seven widely distributed urban communities by the Council of Jewish Federations and Welfare Funds, was focused on coordination of services for the chronically ill.[4] Over a period of ten years, Jewish Welfare Federations in each of the seven communities, with roughly comparable social, professional, and economic conditions, had attempted independently to improve and increase cooperation, coordination, or integration of services among Jewish general hospitals, homes for the aged, and family agencies. The results varied from success to complete failure. The research sought to identify significant features in these communities which could reasonably explain the varying results.

[1] Evon Z. Vogt and Thomas F. O'Dea, "A Comparative Study of the Role of Values in Social Action in Two Southwestern Communities," *American Sociological Review*, XVIII (1953), 649.

[2] Robert Angell, "The Moral Integration of American Cities," *American Journal of Sociology*, LVII, No. 1, Part 2 (1951).

[3] Paul A. Miller, *Community Health Action* (East Lansing, Mich.: Michigan State College Press, 1953).

[4] Robert Morris, *Basic Factors in Planning for Coordination of Hospitals and Institutions for Long-Term Care* (New York: Council of Jewish Federations and Welfare Funds, Inc., 1960).

The research method involved retrospective study carried on within three years of the termination of each planning activity. All available records were reviewed, and all key persons in decision-making in each community, both those opposed to specific means of coordination and those in favor, were interviewed in depth. Professional teams conducted the study in each community, each consisting of a social worker (a community organizer) and either a sociologist or a public health physician. The results gathered by four teams were synthesized; conclusions were tested with the research staff and with social workers in each community.

The second study, sponsored by the Ford Foundation, is now administered by Brandeis University and is concerned with community organization in the field of aging carried on in twelve widely separated communities. The objective of this research is to determine what common features are associated with successful or unsuccessful efforts to meet new needs of the aged. The essential questions are: Can existing resources be mobilized to do more to meet new needs without the creation of new facilities? Is it possible to identify any limits to the wider use of existing resources or the potentiality for their expansion to meet new needs?

The Ford project involves two sample groups. Five urban communities each with a well-established welfare council constitute one group. They have somewhat similar economic characteristics and a similar range of existing services. There are variations among the communities in the general level of private philanthropic support and in the level of professional development among the agencies. The other group consists of seven communities—six counties in a rural area of Minnesota and a single rural county in Kansas. The rural counties lack voluntary welfare councils, but state or local public welfare departments have taken leadership for general community planning and are treated as the community planning organizations.

In all the communities, funds were made available to six of the twelve communities for the local employment of a trained community organizer who devotes full time to the development of resources for the elderly among the existing agencies. (The remaining six, all Minnesota counties, are served as a unit by one community organizer.)

Each community organizer carries on a demonstration of community organization methods and also provides the research staff with current records that follow a specified outline. These data include among other information: details of the project objectives and changes in the objectives; the project director's working plans; the sponsoring organization's general planning for the aging; identification of agencies to be affected by the planning; analysis of the characteristics and interrelationships of members of governing boards of agencies selected as targets for the planning; identification and analysis of community leadership for general planning; and "before-and-after" studies of the characteristics of individuals who are receiving services from selected agencies. (The analyses of consumer characteristics is concerned with older persons who were using selected agency services at the beginning of the project and will be doing so at its close.) Certain general community background data of a socioeconomic character are also being assembled for all communities. Each local community organizer provides the research staff with a bimonthly record of his professional activities.

In addition, teams provided by the research staff visit

each community twice a year to observe local developments and make an objective report that supplements the local professional staff record. Finally, the project directors meet with the research staff annually to review common problems of community planning for the elderly.

The Council and Ford studies have been guided by one aim. There has been no attempt to develop a universal theory of community planning or community organization which is presumed to apply in all situations. Instead, the scope of the study has been narrowed as much as possible. This means that the whole field of community organization has been viewed as consisting of characteristic subareas as far as objectives are concerned. It has been assumed that all community organization programs can be classified as to objectives such as: to achieve closer cooperation between existing agencies to meet new needs; to create new resources to meet new needs either with or without the cooperation of existing resources. Each research deals with one such objective, on the assumption that the dynamic factors which help or obstruct planning for cooperation between two agencies are quite different from the dynamics of creating a completely new resource. The characteristics of leadership, the influences to be dealt with, and the tools available for action may vary according to the objective.

Certain general considerations about the conduct of these intercommunity studies may be of interest.

Community comparability.—A basic question obviously must be: Is it possible to treat a number of communities as really representing a sample? And, if they are a sample, of what? Even if it is theoretically possible, have we the means to locate several communities which have sufficient comparability to permit their treatment as a reasonable sample?

To what extent does the unique history of each community frustrate the effort?

Our studies convince me that communities have similarities as well as differences and that it is possible to balance out a traditional concentration upon unique difference by attention to similarities. In both the Council and the Ford projects it was possible to select certain conditions or factors which by experience or observation were believed to be significant and within certain broad limits to select communities which represented either these factors or variations of them.

Seven urban communities were selected for the Council study, which limited itself to planning by certain Jewish agencies. The general economic conditions in each community could be reasonably compared. The level of philanthropic or public support of welfare services under study could be compared. The levels of community support for social welfare could be roughly compared. The range of services for the chronically ill could be identified and was standardized for the seven communities, although the quality of service could not be standardized. The timing of planning acts could be held reasonably comparable. Local planning for the chronic ill had been done in the five to seven years immediately after the Second World War. In this period, all agencies serving the chronically ill in all parts of the country were subject to common social and technological influences such as the wartime limitation on new construction and advances in medical techniques. Finally, each group of agencies was rooted in a common ethnic and religious community.

In the Ford project, the problem of community comparability is more complex because of the more complicated goals. Here, the study is not carried on among agencies with a common sectarian, ethnic, or religious foundation. A more diverse sample was necessary. The purpose is to study the effect of assigning seven professional community organization workers who would devote full time to organizing services for the aging. They are employed by seven planning agencies which serve the twelve communities: five of them voluntary, welfare planning councils; two of them, public welfare departments. Five of the workers are located in urban communities, all of them with welfare councils; two are in rural areas and work through public welfare departments. The same range of services is needed in all communities although the volume varies. The pattern for financing services for the elderly could be reasonably well standardized for all communities. In all of them, planning mechanisms have been in existence for several years, but only in one instance had there been a paid professional staff assigned to work primarily in the field of aging.

The identification of key variables.—The variables which influence the outcome of planning activities are almost infinite, and it must be confessed that in the present state of our knowledge, these cannot be completely identified, standardized, or in any way controlled by intercommunity study. However, a start can be made to deal with limited numbers of variables and, at least, to derive preliminary conclusions as to their effect on the outcome. In some instances these variables can be identified from preliminary reconnaissance and planned for in the study. In other instances, it has been necessary to fall back on the much less satisfactory device of identifying variables retrospectively and drawing rather loose conclusions from this identification.

In the Council study, the variations in local history were

studied with reasonable care. It was possible to classify communities as having had successful or unsuccessful planning experience. Since the outcomes were different, the method of record analysis and intensive interviews with key people did lead the research staff to certain agreed-upon conclusions about key variables which accounted for the differing outcomes. While the study does not claim that one set of variables leads to success and the other to failure, at least the research does suggest a manageable set of hypotheses which can be tested in the future. The following characteristics were identified as significant in distinguishing the successes from the failures.

1. The simultaneity of organizational crisis in the agencies to be coordinated.

The conclusion from this is that when the object of planning is to bring two agencies into closer cooperation or coordination, success is more likely when both agencies have been badly shaken by an internal or external crisis at about the same time.

2. The informal relationships between trustees of the agencies to be coordinated.

When the trustees of agencies have close social, economic, or political associations with each other of an informal character, success seems more likely than if the trustees move in quite independent circles.

3. The role of leadership.

For purposes of coordination, the research concluded that the decisive leadership characteristic to achieve coordination was twofold: (*a*) the acceptability of the chosen planning leadership to the parties to be coordinated; (*b*) the capacity of this leadership to bridge the conflicting aspirations of the agencies to be brought together. This latter capacity included a readiness to satisfy part of the aims of each organization while at the same time trying to satisfy a wider community goal.

Other variables which emerged had to do with the history of the central planning structure, the role of professional leadership, the use of expert studies, and the use of incentives to encourage adoption of a particular course of action.

Admittedly, this means of identifying variables is unsatisfactory. All that can be claimed is that several teams of researchers working with the central lay and professional persons in seven similar planning situations were able to agree retrospectively about essential features which distinguished success from failure. There may well be a host of other circumstances which did not come into the orbit of study which really accounted for the differing outcomes. This finding is offered primarily to suggest that the method of study can be further refined and developed and offers promise for working out a more exacting theory.

The Ford project is an example of an attempt to correct to a very limited extent some of the deficiencies of the Council project. In all twelve communities, the past history of planning generally and planning for the elderly specifically was available at the start. Certain comparisons within the sample are made possible because two small groups make up the total sample: an urban group with a voluntary welfare council and a rural group with a public welfare department. In all, there is the uniform factor of the newly introduced, skilled, full-time community organization worker. In addition, certain systematic data are being secured from each community during the life of the project on questions which were identified in the Council project. These data include among others:

1. Specification of the objectives of the particular project on aging and the objectives of the sponsoring organization, which in each case is a planning body

2. Significant information about the decision-making board leadership of each of the agencies involved in the planning process

3. Information about the decision-making leadership in the general welfare community and its relationship to the decision-making leadership of the agency serving the elderly

4. Information about the characteristics of users of services at the beginning and the end of each demonstration project.

In addition, certain current data about the activities of each professional project director will be collected and checked by the research observers who visit the communities at intervals.

The range of unspecified influences will still be enormous. At best, we can say that for some dozen factors we will have current data uniformly collected. These can be correlated with various outcomes even if we cannot claim universal proof of cause and effect.

Problems of community selection.—All research of this kind is thus far retrospective in character with all the biases which this introduces. We are not yet able to locate a number of communities which are planning to take certain actions and to set up a research plan which will begin with the action rather than follow after it. As a matter of fact, research of this character labors under a significant disadvantage in that there is insufficient national data by which research personnel can learn what is being planned in enough different places to select an ideal sample.

Even if data were nationally available about activities in

a large number of communities early enough to make proper selection, there remains the difficulty of community willingness to lend themselves for study. The very pace and tempo of planning are such that few communities are prepared to slow down enough to permit the planning of research while they are carrying on their planning for action. Even more serious is the fear of most community leadership that research of this character is likely to upset or disturb the delicate process of negotiation and bargaining which takes place in most planning. The communities which are concerned with serious problems are also likely to be most sensitive about the outcome and reluctant to expose their deficiencies. As a matter of fact, many of them welcome research only when they are quite proud about what the results will show. All that can be said at the present time is that the risk of bias in this type of study can be recognized and to some extent guarded against in the conclusions that are drawn.

Despite these weaknesses, the experience of both the Council and Ford projects indicates that workable samples, at least for experimental purposes, can be assembled successfully. It is important to note that this kind of effective assembling is probably possible only through the cooperation of some national association of social agencies. In the one study, the Council of Jewish Federations provided the essential link of communication between large numbers of communities and an active channel for assembling basic data for choosing a sample. In the Ford project, the efforts of Brandeis University, which served as a collecting point for inquiries and applications, were substantially supplemented by the network of information and communication provided by United Community Funds and Councils, the National

Council on Aging, and the National Social Welfare Assembly.

In both research projects, attempts were made to minimize as much as possible the biases which have been encountered. In the Council project, every effort was made in each community to locate opposing and antagonistic viewpoints among the local leadership and professional staffs. Secondly, outside research personnel was employed for interviewing. Each planning agency agreed to give the research staff complete and uninhibited access to all confidential record data, including correspondence. Data finally assembled and evaluated by the research staff were checked with competent local professional personnel. In the Ford project, the community organizers employed by the seven local planning agencies have reasonably uniform professional backgrounds. These locally employed project directors were oriented in advance to the purposes of the study. In addition, the panel of three Brandeis University observers who visit and observe developments in each community are less involved in local affairs and provide an additional interpretation of local events. All data are assembled during the local planning rather than after the fact.

Problems of definition.—Our research is beset by indefiniteness in even the most basic terms we use. In the Council project, "success" and "failure" need to be defined, and "social work" too lacks a common definition. We found planning goals to be so broadly conceived that results could not be measured objectively. Thus, while one goal is "more coordination," that which constitutes coordination is not defined.

The research staff devised a rough definition of "success" as follows:

Alteration of specified working relationships between two institutions, established as a goal by a community planning organization, adopted by the affected agencies, and operationally effective within ten years of the initial planning. The specified working relationships included major redivision of treatment responsibility, new assignments of personnel, arrangements for transfer of patients, etc. Failure was defined as the inability to agree on a specific plan, lack of agency acceptance, or termination of the plan within ten years. The test used is failure or success of the planning effort, not of the coordination.

Our own definition is less important than the fact that such definitions must be devised by the research, and are not inherent in the phenomena being studied.

Accessibility of Data.—The two projects suggest that studies of community organization and planning cannot in any sense rely upon the written record. Analysis of correspondence, memoranda, and minutes has also proved unsatisfactory as the main method of study, although the written record does provide an initial framework for other methods of analysis. The written record also furnishes a limited check on the memory of persons interviewed. In the Council project, the examination of the written record identified the sequence of certain key actions and also opened up a series of questions about each of these actions. This result was used as the basis for drawing up interview outlines and proved essential in focusing the interviews in all cases.

Perhaps more difficult is the matter of handling the sensitive and controversial material which is usually involved in every important planning activity. The experience of the Council project has been that key people, both professionals and laymen, will talk freely *after the fact,* especially if the interviewers are competent and their questions probing and incisive. There are reasons for believing that it would be much more difficult to secure similar freedom of response during a critical planning period. There are wide indications that key leaders have a keen sense of responsibility for the decisions they are making and are frequently reluctant to talk freely, especially to strangers, for fear of upsetting the local course of events.

With these limitations it can be said that, once interested in research of this kind, communities show through their leadership a hopeful interest in the outcome. In the Council as well as in the Ford communities, both board and professional leadership has been most enthusiastic. They have recognized the limitations of their past achievements and they are most eager to learn for the future. As a matter of fact, this attempt to learn for themselves is strengthened by a desire to make a contribution to the country or to the field. In the Council project, six of the seven communities raised no objection to publication of their case data provided that it adequately concealed individual personalities.

Research personnel.—A word needs to be said about the difficulty of locating competent staff experienced both in community organization and in the methods of research. The limited number of persons trained in any research method makes this especially difficult, but so much social work research has been concerned with the individual that community research techniques are little known even by the most skilled staff. In the Council project, the research staff consisted of a mixture of social workers with community organization experience, sociologists, and public health workers. The results gathered by these teams were checked with local social work personnel as to the facts but not as to the interpretation. It is interesting to note, however, that the interpretations of the research teams were in every instance except one wholeheartedly accepted by the local community organization staff. In several instances, the research staff was informed that their findings provided unexpected insight to the local professional leadership. As a result of the Council's experience, the Ford project is relying more heavily upon social work personnel supplemented only by a certain amount of social science thinking at the planning stage.

Costs.—The cost of research of this type is obviously great. So little is now allocated for fundamental research in local communities that it is not surprising that even less is available for intercommunity study, important though it may prove to be. The Council project is estimated to have cost over a four-year period approximately $250,000. It must be pointed out, however, that the study of community organization process was only one part of a much larger study which resulted in fifteen separate reports on many aspects of chronic illness. It is doubtful if staff, and thus the data, could have been assembled except as part of such a larger enterprise, although there may well be more economical ways of mounting research of this character.

It seems clear that intercommunity research must depend upon national financing. Local contributions of dollars or of personnel are not yet sufficient. Perhaps a time will come when local staffs, sharing a common interest, can pool their talents for such study. Even then there will be required some national fund to employ research planning or coordinating staff. Perhaps national agencies will, in time, provide leadership as a part of their regular operations.

The Ford project, extending over a period of four years, will involve the expenditure of approximately $300,000, of which $220,000 is primarily for the professional staff and $80,000 for the research itself.

The use of control groups.—As has already been indicated, the present research has been satisfied with trying to establish the existence of certain relationships between a few variable factors and certain outcomes. More satisfactory research undoubtedly could be carried forward if projects could be studied in certain experimental communities and observations carried on simultaneously in certain control communities. Unfortunately, the practical means for organizing communities along these lines have not yet presented themselves. Theoretically, it should be no more difficult to assemble a panel of control communities than it is to assemble a panel of experimental or demonstration communities. As a matter of fact, the Ford project at one point contemplated study of developments in several communities comparable to the ones finally selected, but without any professional personnel assigned specifically for work with the aging. The communities could have been selected because they represented the same range of local circumstances as is found in the twelve demonstration communities. However, stringent limitations in financing made this impossible.

Research results.—Certain results can be drawn from the Council project, but the Ford program is still in its early stages. I think the primary conclusion from these two projects is that it is feasible to treat groups of communities as a research sample. Study along these lines does seem to give promise of identifying variables which are associated with differential outcomes in the community organization process. As a result, the method seems to promise a new way to provide the foundation for the next push ahead in the development of theory. From an operational point of view, the research seems to give some hope of reducing the number of key variables which need to be identified in certain categories of planning operations. Of course, the effectiveness of this reduction will depend upon future testing of the preliminary conclusions drawn from the Council project. Finally, it is possible to suggest that studies along these lines may ultimately lead to the development of methods for predicting the outcome of community organization efforts. This will come, of course, when hypotheses are not only drawn from field experience, but are tested.

Even if these more ambitious goals are not really borne out in the future, certain conclusions may be useful. Let me illustrate by selecting only two. First, from the Council project has come certain evidence that the informal relationships among trustees of agencies seem to play an especially important part in planning for coordination.

The second illustration is drawn from the early findings of the Ford project. Social welfare is assumed to have certain objectives for planning. Much of our literature stresses the social work values which characterize social welfare objectives. The Ford findings suggest that a serious deficiency in planning is found in the global and generalized character of social work objectives. In effect, we are finding that planning operations even as well defined as those designed to improve the volume and quality of services for the elderly are usually left at the general level of "we want to improve services for the elderly." This broad objective is seldom translated into specific goals. Such operational objectives mean that precise services are chosen as required and that specific agencies are selected to offer these services, or specific new programs are defined under specified auspices. If this failure to translate broad objectives into operational objectives is borne out by further study, we would seem to have confirmed an important explanation for the deficiencies of certain planning operations which may be corrected by future action.

On the whole, it can be hoped that the tantalizing opportunities opened up by these two pieces of research will lead others to organize similar projects of an intercommunity character. Only if we move in some such direction will we ultimately be able to evolve a penetrating body of community planning theory based on tested experience.

PHYSICAL AND SOCIAL PLANNING

by W. C. Dutton, Jr.

THE PROBLEMS OF PLANNING for concerted action in an individualistic and freedom-loving society continue to be as challenging as the solutions are elusive and mysterious. One might ask why the urban physical planner or the social planner should offer to work with his counterparts in other fields when he himself admits to vast ignorance of what is going on in twentieth-century Western metropolitanism and has had so little success in getting what he has wanted through existing processes of government and private action.

Perhaps that is just the point. There is evidence of a strong concern for synthesizing various aspects of knowledge which have been extended in many directions through intensive work in specialized fields. Possibly we can pool our knowledge and our ignorance, our successes and our failures, and create a larger, more cohesive enterprise. We know far too little of what we should have in our cities and we will, in large part, be dictated to by massive economic and cultural forces. We will have to find a mechanism, an organization, to bring together the many different groups and disciplines that have major concern about the city.

In discussing the obstacles to, and experiments in, social and physical planning at the local level I prefer to think in terms of problems, but problems which in themselves create opportunities for future changes. First, we must recognize that any effort properly to relate social and physical planning is complex and that possibly there has been insufficient analysis as to just what types of relationships should exist. Certainly, some of the programs that are important to social workers will receive little benefit from, and be of slight interest to, urban planners. The reverse likewise is true in that much of the unglamorous work of planning agencies is of relatively little interest to social workers and planners. But we are mutually concerned with the big questions. While our basic concern is for man, his opportunities, problems, adjustment to urban communities, fulfillment, our immediate concern is with the problems of men in their relationship to our urban communities of today and tomorrow. We have to consider this problem within the framework of governmental and nongovernmental organizations and the private actions which affect community change and development. We also have the problem of a differentiated culture in which one uniform set of goals is not of equal validity to all groups. We operate, happily, in a society which traditionally has great respect for individual freedom and which therefore looks with suspicion on centralized planning. While there are many who recognize that "planning *for* freedom" is necessary, there are many others who create obstacles to any formal planning activity, as the history of our professions indicates.

A further problem we have inherited comes from specialization and the difficulty of communication which results from giving different meanings to the same words and developing concepts which have validity within one group, but which have little meaning for other groups. Nevertheless, there are many signs that we are moving rapidly in the direction of finding mechanisms that will facilitate interdisciplinary or interprofessional approaches to major problems. This approach to interprofessionalism is not without its own hazards, and I refer particularly to legal problems created by protective devices such as professional registration. These devices tend to inhibit growth and the application of knowledge that did not exist at the time the particular registration was achieved.

Fortunately, we have some new allies in our efforts to bring about coordination between various Federal aid programs. Senator Harrison Williams, of New Jersey, has spoken very strongly in favor of doing away with the Balkanization of aid programs. Likewise, the proposals and the leadership of the new Administration suggest that we will have an atmosphere in which coordination is considered desirable rather than to be avoided at all costs.

In our attempts to relate social and physical planning activities, we must become quite specific in determining what kind of planning we want to undertake. There are many similarities in the problems we face, and I refer you to the series of discussions held by the Conference on Individualized Services of the National Social Welfare Assembly in 1960 for more detailed information. They suggest to me the possibility that in individual communities representative planners should come together with specific statements of the activities that are being undertaken by either group and analyze each activity to see what the implications are for the other programs and professions.

Then we must consider the approaches that we use. Our profession has sought to establish long-range comprehensive planning as a fundamental governmental activity to be carried on at all levels of government. This is not true in the social planning field. Likewise, we have sought to have the basic planning financed by governmental funds, while there are efforts to keep social planning within the responsibility of private organizations.

Thirdly, we can look at the various techniques we use. While we are far from satisfied with the physical planning techniques we have today, there have been great growth and change in the art and science of planning over the last fifty years. We are very much concerned with the planning process, with the achievement of comprehensive long-range proposals, with the establishment of desirable forms for urban areas and functional relationships of urban activities, and, more recently, with the development of programing techniques to move us more toward our stated goals.

Within social planning, with the problems of its clients, the diversity of its clients, and the diversity of its programs, it does not appear that similar techniques have been applied, even though they are suggested in studies of planning councils and potential community organization programs. One basis for my comment is found in the *Social Work Yearbook* of 1954, which lists nearly fifty separate topics of social work plus various matters of administration and organization. As I look at this publication, I feel that while there is thorough reporting on a number of different subjects, it shows little concern with the coordination and relationship between various elements of social problems. Physical planners struggle within a fearful framework of intergovernmental relationships, both vertically from the national government to local units and horizontally within metropolitan areas. I assume that social planners must cope with the same situation, as well as with the additional problem of the complex pattern of private organizations which in many cases have built up strong national structures and, possibly, inflexible national policies.

I am impressed by the interest being shown by social workers in a review of the historic differentiation between casework, group work, and community organization. I hope that if revised approaches prove to be more suitable for social workers, they also will make it easier to achieve coordination with physical planning.

How far have we come in identifying our mutual objectives? While there have been a number of individual and incomplete statements, perhaps now there can be a serious effort to state mutual professional goals for cities. Senator Williams has called for a national awakening to "the wretched ugliness and the squalor" of the nation's urban areas. Can we agree that this is a desirable program? An old physical planning objective has been the creation of schools and parks in neighborhood areas free of rapidly moving heavy transportation and vehicles. Can social workers agree that this is a desirable objective, at least in the average circumstance? With the extensive growth expected in our metropolitan areas in the next forty years, there is reawakened interest in the concept of satellite city development with various possible cluster arrangements. Do these have good or bad implications for the problems of interest to social workers? Can we start with general concepts of the desirability of having beauty, utility, and form in urban areas and then attempt to define more specific goals?

Even though answers to these fundamental questions are not available to us at this time, we can make much greater progress in relating the planning for physical structures for individual programs such as those of churches, social agencies, schools, group care facilities, to insure that they fit better into the community pattern.

One very significant activity is the Brookings Institution project, which is trying to bring together physical planners and social scientists and others to share information and attempt to open up lines of communications between these people in a community. Experimental programs now under way in Baltimore and Cincinnati suggest that this effort to bring together people who have not been working together may be most successful.

We have heard of several cities, Detroit in particular, where there has been sufficient interest among social workers and planners to maintain periodical meetings over a period of several years. While their contact has been only in terms of freely talking with each other, groundwork can be laid in this way for closer working relationships. The establishment of the Hull House Training Center is encouraging. The Center provides a meeting place for physical and social planners, and efforts are being made to organize a working conference there in the near future.

Of great promise is the work being done in Indianapolis, where social planning needs are being projected parallel with the development of a physical plan for the city and county. The proposed project in Boston that will bring together on one team a representative social planner and city planner to observe and analyze the city's activities and social work, city planning, urban renewal, is expected to develop additional insights into our mutual interests.

One of the first studies of the possible social effects of a planned community was undertaken recently as a student thesis. Alfred Van Huyck, of North Carolina, studied the influence of the Radburn, New Jersey, development on social behavior. While the area involved is too small to allow many firm conclusions to be drawn, the study illustrates the possibility of organizing more intensive research of this type in the future.

I believe that we often fail to capitalize on past achievements to establish the benefits of working together more closely. For example, the provision of physical facilities, such as public housing projects, usually calls for programing of suitable activities or community organization procedures to gain the full social benefit of the program. In some of the projects operated by the Denver Housing Authority, for example, great stress is being laid upon development of tenant participation in various activities and in provision of adequate recreational facilities and programs for the many resident children. The immediate results of the new policy are most encouraging and impressive in solving some of the previous management problems involved in attempting to improve living conditions.

We are facing today new kinds of problems in which close working relationships are necessary. A number of cities, through their urban renewal programs, have begun to tear up their local skid rows. In many of these cities, some understanding of the social pathology of the neighborhood was obtained beforehand; but we all know that without adequate programing and careful treatment of the problems unearthed, the programs may just be transferring social problems from one area of the city to another when they displace skid row residents.

One of the problems that physical planners working in local governments have traditionally is that of meeting the need for a great deal of planning with very little money.

It now appears that this difficulty may be less serious in the future due to the financial support being given by the National Government. This, in turn, has led to several programs in which we are particularly interested, and which offer potentially significant vehicles for developing close working relationships between physical planners, social planners, economic planners, and others.

The first of these is the Community Renewal Programs (CRP). Through the CRP the Federal Government will make a major financial contribution to local communities for a long-range study of urban renewal needs and the development of a program for total urban renewal. In a number of communities, arrangements are being made for social agency councils or other groups to carry on social needs studies. Out of these should come a battery of efforts, and out of the best efforts of today's practitioners can be formulated theories which can be tested in future operations. In this connection I must mention the rebirth of activity in the settlement and neighborhood house movement. I hope not only that these agencies play a part in the study and establishment of community renewal programs but that their potential usefulness in urban renewal will be thoroughly evaluated.

Secondly, a great deal of money will be spent on physical planning for our metropolitan areas. The valuable contribution that the Federal aid program has played since its inception in 1954 justifies its continuation, and we expect considerably larger appropriations to be made in coming years. Why would it not be possible to carry on parallel studies of social needs in metropolitan areas, based on the problems identified in Boston, Washington, Richmond (California), and other cities, concurrently with physical planning? Would it not be appropriate for the National Government to finance such activities through the Department of Health, Education, and Welfare, or possibly by means of an amendment to the Housing Act if that is more desirable? The necessary jobs will not be carried out until there is money available for them. No matter how theoretical or impractical some people think most city planners to be, I find that they are very practical about doing the work for which jobs have been created. The result of Federal financial incentives has been to create or strengthen metropolitan agencies in most of our large urban areas; I am sure that there would be similar action if money were available for social planning.

The third particular device is that of the leadership in the National Government itself. The proposed Department of Urban Affairs and Housing can make tremendous contributions just by starting from the standpoint of total concern for urban needs. Various other steps that have been taken by the Administration to achieve coordination of its programs affecting urban areas suggest that even more coordination between programs will be sought and will be acceptable. We are coming swiftly to the time when it will be possible and worthwhile to sweep away the dust that has settled over the activities of the former National Resources Planning Board and again to erect such a structure at the national level to meet today's needs.

With all these programs and mechanisms to create the opportunities for joint work between our professions, as well as with other professions, we shall face no major inhibitions to developing more coordinated programs.

A STATEWIDE COMMUNITY DEVELOPMENT SERVICE

by Quentin F. Schenk

THE HISTORY OF Western civilization is replete with attempts of man to organize his communal life in such a way as to bring maximum satisfaction to all those who reside therein. Plato, St. Augustine, and the English rationalists, to mention a very few, have written about how they believe the ideal community should be organized. In this country, Emerson, Tugwell, and many others have initiated noble experiments to demonstrate how, in the light of the best knowledge available at the time, man might order his communal living in a more effective way.

Not until the end of the Second World War, however, do we find the men of the sciences devoting a substantial part of their energies toward the solution of this age-old problem. Government, private organizations, universities, religious denominations, are all currently experimenting with the development of the best means of implementing the insights of the sciences into effective programs for the improvement of community life.

One of these experiments is taking place at the University of Missouri, which is trying to respond to the educational needs of the people of its state, but within the context of the larger society. This is only a beginning. My statement concerning the Community Development Program at Missouri is a preliminary one. Furthermore, it is incomplete and, necessarily, biased; for I report to you from the perspective of a social worker, a member of only one of a variety of the disciplines that are addressing themselves to this problem. It is my hope, however, that you will obtain an inkling of what we at the University of Missouri believe to be a significant educational experiment in enabling citizens in communities in our state to solve the complex problems which they face.

It hardly bears repeating that our nation is undergoing a drastic reorganization both geographically and socially. Huge concentrations of people in urban complexes with areas of depopulation in between seem to be the pattern for the future. In the state of Missouri, with just over four million people, more than one million live in the three counties in the St. Louis area, nearly one million in the four counties in the Kansas City area, with the remaining million and one half living in the other 107 counties. New residential areas and new businesses are springing up very fast around these two centers of population, whereas in the hinterland one sees empty houses, empty places of business, vacant school buildings, unused chuches, and ghost villages in the making.

Centralization of services proceeds with centralization of population. In the rural areas the local school district has given way to the reorganized district; school boards with the same number of members as before serve much larger geographical areas than were encompassed in the traditional local district. A central denominational church serves a number of communities instead of one church being located in each community as before. Production and distribution of goods are being centralized as well. Since employment opportunities may no longer exist in the local communities, people must go where the jobs are, which usually means to the city. In the rural areas the traditional forms of government have lost the population and tax base which they were developed to serve. In the larger centers of population the problems and demands far outstrip the governments' organizational and fiscal capacities.

Mass communication media have caused considerable boundary violation of the local community. The attention of the citizen is focused more than ever on world problems, on national problems, which consequently lessens his concern for community problems. The control of local policy is shifting from the hands of the "old families" to be shared with other groups, such as management, labor, and some of the well-established professions. This causes disruptions in the policy-making processes in the community. Professionalization itself has tended to erode the concept of lay responsibility. With the increasing complexity of problems, professions and other specialized groups have arisen and now take a good share of the responsibility for the definition and solution of community problems. Thus, the citizen feels bewildered and is less inclined to take responsibility for decisions and action in community affairs. If he does take some of the responsibility, he is likely to turn his attention to the neighborhood, or suburb, which he is more likely to understand than the large city, and over which he feels he has some measure of control. This tends to cause an atomization of the community as a whole.

This fundamental reorganization of our society has produced problems that local communities cannot handle by means of their own resources. Government reports and programs of assistance to local communities, research by such organizations as Community Studies, Inc., of Kansas City, and numerous investigations by universities attest to the fact that help must be given. The volume of requests that we receive at the University of Missouri is additional evidence of this need.

Once the need has been established, next comes the question as to how the problem should be met. Is a professional service required? What agency should field the service? Will more than one agency be involved? What kind of knowledge and skill is required to deal with the problems adequately? What contributions can be made by community-oriented professions such as social work, education, and so on? What further research is needed?

I turn now to the various approaches which are used by agencies that are trying to assist communities with their problems and, in particular, to that used by the University of Missouri.

Approaches to community work.—

1. *Common sense.* When a community requests assistance from an agency, the agency responds with mailed information that usually contains guides for action and anecdotes citing how other communities have solved a similar problem. If personnel from this type of agency get in touch with the community, their job will be primarily to motivate the community to action, and then leave it to its own resources. Agencies that advocate this approach generally assume that the main problem is apathy, lack of desire, and that once the motivation is furnished, the community can fall back upon its own previous experience and solve the problems which it is facing. Oftentimes, however, harking back to use of common-sense previous experience for the

solution of a particular problem can only aggravate it. This is not to deny the fact that information can be useful in finding a solution.

2. *Single interest.* The agency tends to list all problems of the community in a single category. The most typical example of this in recent years has been the assumption that all community problems can be considered economic in nature. This is not to say that production and distribution of goods are not vital to the community, but it must be remembered that economic problems are merely one of the major types which people face. Other agencies tend to assume that all major community problems can be solved by setting up a formal organizational structure to get people "involved." If enough people are busy with an organization that deals with community problems, somehow an adequate solution will be found. Involvement indeed is important, but this again is only one aspect of the situation.

3. *Analytical.* The agency that uses this approach assumes that when all the facts are known by the people who have the problem, intelligent action will follow automatically. The many specialized agencies that conduct surveys in various aspects of community planning fall into this category. It need not be further documented here how many of these expert analyses gather dust on the shelves of our agencies and governmental offices and are never used. Once again, information which oftentimes only experts can gather is very important to the proper action in the solution of community problems, but by no means is it the entire answer.

4. *Integrated.* The agency that employs this approach seeks to use the many strong aspects of the other approaches, but yet goes a bit further. In the integrated approach, the

procedures previously discussed are not seen as ends in themselves, but as procedural means to move toward the most crucial aspects of the whole problem, its solution. Anecdotes, information, conceptualization of problems around a function of the community, skilled analysis, are all separate but yet related means to assist the people in the community to solve their problems. The focus of this approach is constantly on the action which is to be taken by the people in the situation to reestablish the equilibrium which was upset by the onset of the problem.

In this approach four components of the situation are considered to be in constant interaction: the physical environment; the social-cultural situation; the community worker; and the people in the community. Because of the diversity and complexity of the situation, a wide variety of resources and skills is needed. It follows that an interdisciplinary, interagency approach is required if this plan can be utilized. It also follows that among the specialists required there must be at least one skilled practitioner who comprehends the interworking of the four major components. This worker must understand how to analyze the problem in terms of these major components, how each one affects the creation of the problem, and how they can be used to effect a solution to it. He must understand the potentials and limitations of each component and the possible techniques that might be used to solve the problem. He must be able to work with the people in the situation, using his general knowledge to deal with each instance; for while each has the same elements, the interrelationship of these elements alters from situation to situation, as well as within each as movement takes place.

When a request for service comes to an agency that uses

this integrated approach, the worker skilled in the understanding and use of the social processes must be prepared to work with the people with the problem from start to finish, bringing to bear the multiple resources at his disposal—his own skill, the skill of other specialists, outside resources, the wealth of human and physical resources that exist in the community. This is a highly skilled task which cannot be performed unless the worker is highly trained in the intricacies of the field.

The Community Development Program at the University of Missouri is working to make effective this approach to community problems. In a sense, we are experimenting with transferring the skills of social work which have been directed primarily toward the development of social policy as it affects individual well-being to the development of services which will assist in social policy formulation and social action to bring about well-being at the community level.

The worker in the community.—Sociologists are contributing much to the understanding and definition of corporate functions and common needs in communities, and are showing us how to identify them. We can describe systematically how people organize themselves in communities to make and to spend money, to raise and educate their young, to meet their religious needs, and so on. An understanding of this highly stylized, predictable way in which people organize to carry out these corporate functions is of utmost importance to the community worker in helping him determine his own helping role.

It should be apparent that it is no easier to define a community than it is to define an individual human being or a primary or secondary group. The component parts of communities which are organized to meet common needs have been variously described as functional units, or institutions. However they are called, they are a series of complex relationships which carry rewards or penalties for the persons who function in these relationships, depending upon how they execute their expected performance. Now, these kinds of relationships are seemingly almost self-operating, and oftentimes they change very slowly. So a person from outside the community who is bent on altering prescribed ways of doing assigned tasks in that community, has a complex, difficult task on his hands.

An example will illustrate the situation. We have much more leisure time now than we ever have had, and many communities are struggling to organize activities so that people can use this time constructively. Suppose that the money-making social units in a community decide that recreational programs, privately run and supported by fees, plus commercial recreational establishments, such as bowling alleys, private parks, and so on, offer the best solution of this problem. On the other hand, suppose that the money-spending social units in the community feel that participation in recreational activities should be based on considerations other than the ability to pay for them, and advocate a diversified, public-supported program. Now, it is easy to see that there is a highly complex series of social relationships among the money-making units which influenced the formulation of their policy. The same holds true for the money-spending units. If only commercial recreational programs materialize, it is clear that the money-making units of the community are the most powerful; the reverse might also be true. In reality, compromises are usually arrived at, because of the obvious balance needed between making and spending, in relation both to resources and to cultural values.

If these component parts of a community are having difficulty in working out satisfactory relationships, and thus social policy is made by default and hence is unsatisfactory to almost everyone in that community, some outside aid might be needed. Decisions are made by persons in communities not only in reference to the values held by the subunits of the local area, but also in reference to what is prescribed as proper community behavior by the larger society. So, a request might go out to the state university for assistance with the development of a recreation program. The request usually comes from one of the community units, such as the money-spending or the money-making unit, but not usually from both. One of the problems of the situation might be the relationship between these two units.

The approach advocated by University of Missouri community organization specialists concentrates upon the structuring of the relationships among the various units of the community in relation to the problem at hand. We assume that if the relationships are developed properly in regard to a given problem, the solution will be to the best interests of the community. Thus, in relation to the recreation program, the worker, upon request from the community, would try to: (1) understand the situation from the standpoint of the various units that see it as a problem; (2) bring all available information to bear upon the problem so that it could be considered as rationally as possible; (3) persuade the various units concerned, or those that should be concerned, to work together to find a common approach or policy; and (4) then help them put the policy into action. The emphasis here is upon what the community does and how it does it, not on what the final outcome will be, important as this is.

Thus, community organization might be defined as follows by those who have been primarily concerned with it at the University of Missouri: Community organization is that professional service to a local area which, first, attempts to further effective relationships among the social units in that area in reference to the solution of a common problem or problems; and, second, attempts to make more effective the adjustability between the community and the larger society.

The latter portion of this definition recognizes the important fact that communities, like other social units, do not function in a vacuum, but within the framework of a larger society which sets limits, prescribes alternative modes of behavior, and furnishes resources which can be utilized by communities as they organize themselves to meet human need. It bears reemphasizing that the community organization specialist is only one resource, one of many types of specialists needed in communities to help identify and solve their complicated problems.

Again using recreation as an example, if it is decided that a public program is essential, someone who understands the local legal issues, as well as state and Federal regulations, will need to counsel with the persons who are working for this type of program. An expert in facilities might be needed rather than a "social process" specialist. Someone who understands programing in reference to age groupings should be consulted. Occasionally, one individual can function in both capacities. It is important to understand that at certain stages in this whole problem-solving process technical specialists are needed, and it is the responsibility of the community worker to locate these specialists and bring them into consultation when they are needed.

If this definition be accepted, it follows that the community worker must be: (1) a student of social organization; (2) acquainted with the subject matter approaches to community problems, perhaps even be proficient in one of them; and (3) skilled in dealing with problems of the structuring of the elements and dimensions of a community.

The agency in the community.—Public universities have long had a tradition of educational service to many groups of people in their respective states, not only to the students who come to the campuses for formal education. Both general extension and agricultural extension have provided adult education for many decades, and it is in this tradition that the Community Development Program was born at the University of Missouri. The Program began in 1957 in the general extension portion of the off-campus educational services of the university. In 1960, however, the University of Missouri integrated its extension services into one University Extension Division in which the general extension and agricultural extension services are now a single unit. Therefore, the Community Development Program can call upon the resources of the entire university.

It should be apparent that the Community Development Program is oriented at the level of the total community not merely of a segment of the community, which has been the historic approach of most of the professions which are concerned with community action programs. For instance, social work has been historically concerned with the so-called "welfare" community; agricultural extension, with the "agricultural" community; and general extension, with the "educational" community. Because of this tradition, steps were necessary to prevent locking the Community Development Program to a single segment of the community; but much progress is being made that will permit its continued orientation to the total community. This is not to say that the other programs are not important; but we believe that a number of the problems of our society must be attacked at the level of the total community by a professional group, while other problems must still be attacked at the level of the functional or special-interest community by other programs.

The Community Development Center combines three efforts, those of research, education, and extension. Up to this point there has been little clarification of the role of research in this field or of how formal education should be used in the training of community workers. The extension arm of the program is the one most clearly established at this time.

The University Extension Service contains two types of personnel—administrative personnel and program specialists. The major categories of administrative personnel are the directors, the state agents, and the county agents. These men are responsible at their various levels for formulation of fiscal policy and for the administration of general program policy.

Program specialists also exist at the state and county levels. In the field of community development the specialists who operate at the state level generally function as educators, helping the local agents to develop proper programs in the same fashion that the supervisor works with the social worker in the social agency. In addition, the program specialists at the state level have the responsibility for resource furnishing, both within the university and around the state as a whole. That is to say, if the local agent who is working with a community on a particular problem finds that resources are needed that he cannot lay his hands upon locally, he would call upon the state community development specialists to help him locate them. Such a resource might be an engineer from the university, a consultant from the medical school, a consultant in government, or someone from the state medical society or from the State Division of Resources and Development. The state agent in conjunction with the local community development agent would discuss with these resource persons when and how their talents might be used in consultation with the community.

The local community development agent is responsible administratively to the county agent, who was formerly the County Agricultural Extension Agent. The duties of this agent are being modified from those of a generalist in agricultural matters to those of a more local administrator of a wide variety of programs—not only the old traditional agricultural ones but also new ones, such as the Community Development Program and others formerly fielded by the general Extension Service of the University.

So far, the University has placed five community development agents in the field. Plans call for programs in Kansas City and St. Louis, one agent being assigned to the St. Louis metropolitan complex and another to the Kansas City metropolitan complex, with the possibility of additional agents who will give direct services to these areas. The details of this program have not yet been worked out, but a study is being made of the possible ways in which the whole concept of community development can be tied in to the large differentiated pattern which we find in these two parts of our state.

Obviously, one agent will not be able to deal with the total community, as is possible in a small rural or medium-sized community; this would be an impossible task in an area containing one or two million people. Also, the community development agent would have to become much more specialized in the urban setting. He would be dealing more specifically with the organizational problems involved in a functional area of the community and he would have to be concerned with a relationship to a team of specialists rather than with the general type of work which he can do in the smaller community.

For instance, there is a possibility that we can place an organizational specialist in the regional health and welfare planning council of one of these two metropolitan areas. This, then, would be his "community," but his responsibility would be to tie his "community" into the workings of the other institutional sections of the metropolitan area and also to attempt to tie this health and welfare institutional complex in with the university services and other resources of the state at large. Emphasis in the large metropolitan areas would have to be placed upon highly competent research to a much greater extent than is necessary in the rural and middle-sized communities of Missouri. We hope that experiments which are going on in the Ford Foundation projects in Wisconsin and New Jersey will contribute toward the clarification of the role of the urban agent so that these concepts can be utilized as the University of Missouri attempts to develop services to the urban portions of the state.

Implications for social work.—Growing out of our experience in the Community Development Program at the University of Missouri are implications that we believe to be of importance to social work:

1. Social work should reevaluate its professional role to see if it is concentrating upon that portion of the social system most crucial to the efficient functioning of the society. The profession of social work is in many respects unique; especially so is the fact that it is the only action-oriented group which holds as its central concern man in relation to society, and attempts to develop professional services to assist men to create and maintain adequate, constructive, helpful relationships with their fellow men.

The great reformers of the nineteenth century, the pioneers in our field, were concerned with the structure of society primarily because it was related to opportunities for the economically disadvantaged and the unassimilated immigrant groups in a young America. Shortly after the turn of the century the normative pattern of the profession concentrated upon the individual and his relationships with his environment. To be sure, social group work reflected the realization of the profession that problems can be generated and solved at the group level, but this has never been the primary concern of the profession. Also, there has been a movement within social work toward the attack on, and solution of, problems in the social unit called the "community," but up to this point the profession's concentration upon community organization has been concerned primarily with the organization of this social unit to provide the resources necessary to maintain the traditional, individually oriented services.

It has been pointed out that this individually oriented service may be a luxury which our society cannot afford; that society will not be able to provide helping services for all individuals who might need them; and that somehow individual problems will need to be dealt with in a larger context. Moreover, there are some of us in the profession who view this concept in a different theoretical framework. Some of us hold that today's social problems are not primarily individually oriented, but that they are primarily oriented at the level of community; that the focal point of forces which provide for the socialization of the individual and for the maintenance of social control is found not in the family, not in the group, but in the community. We hold that a new approach to our pressing problems is necessary, that we must reorient our attack and concentrate it upon the community. This is not to say that services to individuals or groups are not necessary, but only that a rethinking of the helping process, in relation to its focal point of service, is definitely in order.

2. The direct-service method of social work for assisting individuals and groups can be applied to the community unit as well. To be sure, the profession cannot claim the entire field of community service as its own prerogative. Many professions, many disciplines, have a contribution to make, both in a basic and in an applied sense. However, social work through its years of clinical experience in dealing with the problems of man in relation to society has a unique contribution to make; and this contribution is in the area of guiding the development of relationships among the community elements. Sociologists, anthropologists, economists, and other social scientists can describe what these relationships have been, how they are changing, and what their form generally might take in the future, but social work has had a significant background of experience in the particularization of these relationships in general. Social work has had decades of experience in taking individual theory, group theory, and theory of the community, and

with this training personnel who are capable of helping particular individuals, particular groups, and particular communities to build the types of relationships that are necessary for constructive and beneficial living.

Those of us who have been experimenting in the field of community action are convinced that this generic, helping process is one unique contribution which the social work profession can make, regardless of the nature of the problem, to assist individuals, groups, and communities as they work out their destinies. Social work has long concentrated on the concept of the individual as being in a dynamic relationship with his environment; of the group as being made up of individuals in a dynamic series of relationships; and of the group as a whole having a definite relationship with the larger society. This same kind of conceptualization should now be applied to communities—that a community is not only a geographical area; that a community is not only an identifiable series of organizational structures confined to a local area; that it is one of the three basic units of society. This is to say that a community is a social unit just as a group or an individual is a social unit, and that it has component parts just as do groups and individuals. To be sure, these component parts are different from the component parts of the group or of the individual, but the specifics can be dealt with as long as this dynamic concept of interrelationships is kept in mind and the solution of the problem is the focal point.

3. Social work can help develop the team approach to the solution of community problems. The profession has long held that not only does it give direct service, but also it is concerned that all resources that pertain to the solution of a given social problem be brought to bear upon it. Social

work has pioneered in the team approach to problems both at the practitioner and at the agency level.

As we have stated, many disciplines are needed to help provide solutions to community problems. Members of these disciplines must develop their specialized functions as parts of the team. Social workers can function both as subject matter and as process specialists as members of that team. The social worker is a subject matter specialist in many areas of welfare problems, and could be used as a research and educational specialist in this field.

The social worker is a specialist also in initiating and guiding voluntary action, especially in informal relationships. His skill could be used to assist the members of the community to initiate and carry through the process of identification, study, and action regarding their problems, if the self-help process is to be utilized in the attack upon the problems which communities face today. Murray Ross, in his two excellent books, sets forth this thesis as well as it has yet been stated.[1]

It seems very clear that social work skill is needed to help redefine the relationship of the individual to community as dictated by the profound reorganization in which our American society is currently engaged. I am sure that if social work can determine that this is one of its prime functions in our contemporary society, it will rise to the task and help move America toward its destiny.

[1] Murray Ross, *Community Organization, Theory and Principles* (New York: Harper, 1955); Murray Ross, *Case Histories in Community Organization* (New York: Harper, 1958).

THE GREAT CITIES SCHOOL IMPROVEMENT PROGRAM

by Henry Saltzman

THE ROOTS OF the problems of people who live in the core and gray area of our cities reach to the bedrock of our social problems—poverty, poor housing, prejudice, delinquency, transiency, family and neighborhood disorganization. In the array of services and institutions that seek to improve the quality of living in these urban depressed areas, the centrality, if not the primacy, of the schools is clear.

The positive effects of education are obvious. When we can effectively teach the lower-class child, the opportunities for his economic and social improvement greatly increase. This fact alone makes the role of the school of great relevance to all efforts in the gray areas. Of equal importance in assessing the functions of schools is the singular lack of option which the institution of public education has been given. No "case" can be closed for lack of cooperation. No client can be turned away as "obviously unsuited to receive treatment." No building can be closed in order to follow the more desirable clients. The public schools cannot pick and choose; they cannot write off; they cannot retreat.

The public schools, therefore, are one of the most strategically placed staging areas from which to mount vigorous, comprehensive, and preventive programs to achieve the maximum development of much of the human potential lying dormant and unchallenged in our urban slums and gray areas.

I want to make as real as possible to you the problems of the schools involved in the Great Cities–Gray Areas program of the Ford Foundation, and, indeed, of all the schools that serve the poor, the deprived, and the alienated. Let me chart our "sea of troubles" by a reference to two human beings rather than by tables, graphs, or statistical extrapolations.

A year ago, as director of the Bedford–Stuyvesant School in Brooklyn, New York, I was interviewing applicants for a special summer program we were to operate in collaboration with the Institute for Developmental Studies of the Downstate Medical College. We were going to test the effect of a mild tranquilizer on underachieving children enrolled in a program of remedial reading. Lists of such children had been provided by the local public schools, and we sent cards to the parents to inform them of the program.

Among the first to appear for an interview were Mrs. Annie Duncan and her son Johnny. I learned that Mrs. Duncan had been born in a small rural Mississippi town; she had never gone to school and was illiterate; she had eight children living with her; she had never been married; and she was receiving welfare assistance.

After listening to an explanation of the nature of the program, and agreeing to let Johnny participate, Mrs. Duncan had to sign a permission slip to allow the administration of the drug. Without thinking, I pushed a pencil and the form across the desk to her.

The woman was transfixed. She began to tremble visibly. Perspiration beaded her forehead. Forcing herself, she reached spasmodically for the pencil—and missed, gouging a sliver of wood from the desk top with her fingernail.

Mrs. Duncan finally signed the paper. Johnny, who was ten and already three years below his grade level in reading, attended classes and improved in his reading ability.

It is not difficult for social workers to conjure up an image of Mrs. Duncan's life—its drabness, its unrelieved poverty, its unremitting isolation from culture, beauty, comfort, its meager and ofttimes immoral or unhealthy consolations. And yet, from this morass, emerged a mother willing to undergo the agonies of exposure in order to push her child's education along.

The schools engaged in our program recognize that Johnny cannot be the sole target of our effort nor the sole participant in the program. We recognize that the Johnny Duncans, the Johnny Gonzales's, the Johnny Whitefeathers, and the Johnny Calhouns are caught in a tempest of family and community forces that impinge on their learning abilities and negate and diffuse the schools' efforts. Thus, we must extend our program beyond the schoolchild to reach the parents, *their* peer groups, and improve the social and cultural climate of the neighborhood.

Professional workers in other fields often raise this question when a school man outlines broad social objectives for school programs which go beyond the formal education process: "Is this expanded role a proper one for the public school?" We have certainly been lambasted by spokesmen from without as well as from within our guild for "neglect" of our job, which is to train the mind. We have, in effect, been told to leave social work to the social workers and get back to teaching.

Let us try to settle this matter by recognizing that while

we have one board of education in our cities, we have two school systems or, perhaps more accurately, two communities of schools. One of these communities consists of the "steady schools"—steadily attended by children who are steadily improving their learning performance and who are steadily supported by parents who, in turn, steadily adhere to American middle-class standards. For such a community of schools, learning *is* the first order of business.

The second community of schools is the one rapidly expanding in our core and gray areas. In these schools we find high rates of pupil transiency (as much as 100 percent in some), large numbers of students who perform considerably below grade level in reading and arithmetic, serious classroom behavior problems, a variety of health problems that affect learning capacities, very high drop-out rates, large numbers of subject failures, poorly motivated pupils, many emotionally disturbed pupils. Among the families of these children we find large numbers of broken homes, chronically unemployed fathers, high disease rates, large families living in the poorest housing facilities, low educational levels, and high adult and infant mortality rates. These conditions are the by-products of impoverished neighborhoods, disorganized and voiceless in the urban community, ripe for demagoguery, and alienated from many of the political and welfare institutions that are able to help them.

So long as we continue to plan for both of these communities of schools as if they were one, we shall, I submit, continue to play a game of educational charades and we shall continue to be frustrated because these schools do not conform to the desired mold. Therefore, I believe it is legitimate for school planners and administrators to go beyond the traditional programs and operate with a different set of priorities if we are ever to move forward with the serious and difficult business of training the minds of lower-class, deprived children.

The forty-one public schools located in Buffalo, Chicago, Cleveland, Detroit, Milwaukee, Philadelphia, Pittsburgh, St. Louis, San Francisco, and Washington, D.C., that are participating in the Great Cities–Gray Areas program [1] all face the complex and distressing syndromes of the problems I have listed. To forge a more effective program, they have established the following set of common concerns above and beyond their traditional educational objectives:

1. The school shall be concerned with the quality of family and community life when it is detrimental to the learning and school adjustment of the child.

2. The school shall realistically assess the kinds of services needed by the slum child and his family and be willing to render these services if other agencies are inadequate.

3. The school shall make a realistic effort to provide programs for adults in basic education and in the facts of urban living so that parents may become more supportive of their children.

4. The school shall actively seek partnerships with the other public and private agencies that are rendering needed services to the gray areas. These partnerships should enable all concerned to do their respective jobs more effectively.

5. The school shall seek ways of involving neighborhood residents more meaningfully and more actively in the program.

6. The school shall be particularly concerned with the

[1] Information concerning the project, the names and addresses of project directors, and other details may be obtained from the Ford Foundation.

in-migrant child and his family and develop better programs to facilitate their urbanization.

7. The school shall provide greater access to cultural, service, and work experiences which will broaden expectations, increase the motivation to learn, and develop suitable skills and attitudes.

8. The school shall put heavier emphasis on the teaching of communication, recognizing the fact that only through skill in reading, writing, speaking, listening, and seeing can one hope to improve one's social, educational, and economic position.

9. The school shall be concerned with the continuing education of teachers because only through their deeper knowledge and greater skill can education ultimately be improved.

10. The school shall recognize that the per pupil dollar cost of educating the deprived youngsters must exceed that spent on the "average" youngster. An effective gray area program is a costly one.

Let me take one of these ten common concerns—the development of active partnerships with other agencies—and describe some of the efforts that are being made. We all know that many such relationships already exist, most strongly and effectively between schools and other public agencies such as a recreation department or the juvenile court. Liaisons between schools and the nonpublic agencies are apt to be irregular, unsustained, and not particularly advantageous to the smaller agency which has an ample case load of nonschool referrals. However, in both cases, it would be safe to say that these communications and interrelationships tend to develop at the needs end of the school program rather than at the planning end. In other words, we turn to other agencies when we need help; we rarely involve them when we are planning new schools or school services.

Over and over again, in our discussions with the school staffs involved in our program, the need for involving other interested agencies that have talents to offer has been stressed. Our school people have been receptive and some interesting events have occurred.

In one city, some twenty-four private agencies, under the aegis of the health and welfare federation, have been meeting with the school staff to explore possibilities of combining agency and school programs in mutually supportive ways. In addition, the county health department is continuing to make expanded and improved services available to the project schools. Local settlement houses and boys clubs have also been consulting with the schools to develop co-operative programs. An urban renewal agency, developing neighborhood conservation and community organization programs in a deteriorating gray area, has been actively discussing with the school superintendent and his staff ways in which the two programs can complement and strengthen one another.

In two cities, the superintendents of schools have called together the commissioners of the municipal agencies as well as the executive directors of private and Federal agencies. The purpose of these meetings was to initiate a process through which an experimental master social plan for a problem area which would involve the redesign of services already present. In each case, direct participation by the chief administrative officer of the city is involved.

In another large city, several group work agencies, long experienced in the neighborhoods served by the project schools, were called upon to conduct workshops and short training sessions with teachers and special project personnel. In addition, an expanded after-school program for children and adults is offering additional opportunities for agency staff to work with parents in less formal settings.

Citizens groups such as block clubs, community councils, and special-interest groups have become interested in a number of cities. In these situations, the indigenous groups were given a thorough briefing on the nature of the schools' effort, and their support and involvement were solicited. In a number of instances, this effort has resulted in direct participation of many citizens in various phases of the school program.

In another city, a settlement house which operates a camping program has offered its facilities for an experiment in educational camping for project pupils.

Another slum community which has organized a number of community councils under the leadership of the health and welfare federation is actively planning with the project staffs ways to make better use of existing facilities toward the end of making all agency programs more effective.

If we in the schools are going to be true to our stated purpose of reaching beyond the child to the parent and the community, these liaisons with other agencies become critically important. Without continuing and mutually supportive interagency programing, we cannot hope to establish the broadest and most effective flow of needed services to the residents of the depressed areas. Without these services, the schools cannot hope to break the vicious cycle by which despair is passed on from generation to generation. While much social work must of necessity continue to be a picking-up-the-pieces operation, this effectively done can purchase for the educator the precious years he needs to teach the child the skills and impress upon him the aspirations which may lead to self-reliant adult living.

As we have gone ahead with our program we have identified a number of new goals toward which we need to move:

1. The development of curricula and teaching techniques to foster the language development of the preschool and kindergarten-age child and an expansion of the day care programs

2. Flexible school programing to allow for the in-service training of teachers

3. The development of more suitable reading materials for lower-class urban children

4. The development in the teacher training institutions of an interdisciplinary approach to the preparation of the urban schoolteacher

5. The expansion of clinical opportunities for future teachers so that they will begin to see the gray area community from different angles—the family service agency, the juvenile court, the settlement house, and so forth

6. The discovery of opportunities for neighborhood residents to participate in the school's program.

These six goals are basically education-oriented. There are two other concerns which have broader significance. First, it is our hope that cities will develop comprehensive social plans for the gray areas—with an investment of energy, staff, money, and political commitment comparable to that now being given to the development of master physical plans.

Secondly, we hope that school construction programs, closely coordinated with urban renewal projects, will be viewed as opportunities to establish community schools, planned in cooperation with community agencies and citizens, which will furnish a neighborhood base for the provision of expanded, more closely integrated services to the gray area and its residents.

The obvious need for comprehensive social planning for the gray areas and the accelerated program of physical reconstruction of these neighborhoods presents a great opportunity. The bricks-and-mortar effort must be accompanied by similar growth in social planning by the people who will be concerned with the children and the adults once they get inside the new facilities.

If social planners can make their voices heard in the councils of the physical planners, I predict that we will have enlightened programs bolstered by the physical facilities which strengthen and enhance social programs.

One approach toward this broader effort might be through the development of community schools. The concept of the community school is not a new one. It has its roots in the neighborhood-based school which services all the children of the community. During the height of foreign immigration to this country, educators saw that a school could perform many tasks which could ease the adjustment of the new arrival to his new country. However, the community school idea faded in the thirties, and only recently has there been any indication of serious effort to revive the idea.

I should like to see a decision on the part of boards of education to make *all* gray area schools—new, old, those still to be built—into true community schools. To do this would involve the active participation of four major groups of urban agencies—the board of education, the Urban Renewal Agency, the social agencies which expend public funds in the gray areas, and the health and welfare council.

These groups are not coequal. Only three are in a position to commit funds and staffs on a long-range basis to the effective planning and operation of community-based programs. The council is strategic, however, because it has the capacity for recommending to its member agencies participation and commitment to the program.

The basic commitment of each agency would be as follows:

The board of education would: (1) select key school staff (principal, community coordinator, guidance coordinator) two years before the new community school is opened; (2) agree to plan the physical structure of the school to follow as closely as possible the recommendations of the planning group; (3) keep the school staff free to participate actively and, during the planning period, on a full-time basis with the other agencies and citizens' groups who will have a share in the community served by this school; (4) make available from its files the data needed by the other agencies to set up coordinated programs.

The housing and redevelopment authority would: (1) make available its community survey data to other agencies; (2) adjust timetables and program objectives to harmonize more closely with the plans of the other agencies; (3) make its professional staff available to the planning group to consider physical plant requirements of the community school; (4) through planning, insure against major dislocation of population which would render null the specific planning of the agencies; (5) modify its construction plans to fit neighborhood needs as these are expressed by local citizens and agencies.

Public agencies would: (1) make staff available for regular consultation and planning; (2) introduce new action programs to meet specific problems; (3) adopt more flexible staffing practices to permit tie-in with other programs.

The health and welfare federation would: (1) survey the gray area to discover which agencies are already making major commitments of time and staff; (2) develop inter-agency programs which give high priority to the areas; (3) insure, if possible, long-term commitments from agencies that they will stay involved in the area.

What might result from such an effort?

1. A school would be built whose facilities would be available for use by social agencies, health agencies, and interested citizen groups on a seven-day-a-week, twelve-months-a-year basis.

2. The staffs of every agency involved would find new and significant roles to play in a number of new settings.

3. Much closer cooperation between schools and agencies would result.

4. Public agency support would be strongly felt by social workers from the voluntary agencies.

5. Fuller sharing of data would be facilitated.

6. There would be a neighborhood base of operations for many centralized agencies.

7. Closer contacts among citizens and agencies would ensue.

8. Preventive programs could more easily be launched.

9. Each institution could establish a closer tie with its neighborhood.

10. A climate of mutual interest among agencies would aid the trial of new programs.

11. Through closer contact with many institutions and agencies, professionals would broaden their understanding and develop more generalized skills than heretofore. Thus,

a new breed of generalists might arise among social workers. This could correct the atomizing effects of the overspecialization now evident.

12. Opportunities for observation of, and communication with, children and adults in a wide variety of situations would open up.

13. All workers would come to have a neighborhood "bias" rather than an agency bias.

Not long ago I listened to the director of a redevelopment authority outline a massive rehabilitation and redevelopment program which would affect every neighborhood and district of a certain city. He spoke of building designs, real estate, population density, and the tax base. At the conclusion of his presentation he was asked if he had any plans for meeting the social needs of the people then living in the deteriorated areas.

His answer was: "I am a physical planner. I have a master plan and I must move quickly. Where is the social planner with his master plan for the city?"

The challenge is blunt, clear, and direct. It speaks to the long-standing fact of fractionalized, diffused, overlapping, uncoordinated, competitive, and wasteful social welfare efforts which characterize our cities in both the public and private sector. We must strive for more efficient use of money, strategic deployment of staffs, imaginative program planning, and integration of effort of public and private welfare. As the schools move forward to improve the education of the children of the gray areas, we fervently hope that this effort will mesh with other programs in a sustained, efficient, and productive partnership.

SERVING YOUTH: A CHILD'S GARDEN OF SOCIAL AGENCIES

by Bertram M. Beck

THERE WERE 10.9 MILLION 14–17 YEAR OLDS in the United States in 1959, an increase of nearly one-third of a million over 1958. Continued increases are expected to bring this number . . . . to . . . . 16.4 million by 1975." [1] If we operate on the assumption that all—or practically all—of our existing services are of equal merit, then we come to the conclusion that each existing service must augment its capacity to serve by more than 50 percent in the next fifteen years. This does not take account of the need for new services that might be engendered by the development of new problems. Nor does it take account of the need to expand existing services as a consequence of an increase in the incidence of the occurrence of certain problems.

Can such a goal for all services be accomplished? Firstly, there is the question of dollars. The U.S. Department of Labor estimates that by somewhere between 1960 and 1970 we can increase production of goods and services by about 50 percent and provide our expanding population with a 25 percent increase in its standards of living.[2] Surely it is

[1] *Young Workers under 18,* 1959 Supplement, Leaflet No. 6 (rev.; Washington, D.C.: U. S. Department of Labor, 1960).

[2] *Manpower—Challenge of the 1960's,* U. S. Department of Labor (Washington, D.C.: U. S. Government Printing Office, 1960), p. 2.

not overly optimistic to assume that we will continue to receive the same proportion of national income for youth services in the decade to come as we have in the decade just past. While there is no precise measure of dollars spent on youth services or on welfare services in general, there is some significance in the fact that Federal expenditures in this general area almost doubled in the last decade.[3] This would seem to lend support to the idea that increasing total population would yield sufficient voluntary and tax support to enable existing services at least to hold the line in the face of increasing youth population. Standing on the new frontier, it does not even seem overly optimistic to suggest that we may even gain from our expanding economy a larger proportion of support and so enlarge somewhat the volume of service and even launch some new services.

The picture, however, is not equally rosy for all types of agencies and services. Viewing the spectrum of services as they appear in the typical community, the keystone is, of course, the school. "Since 1950 the number of school enrolled youth has been steadily climbing. . . . . Continued increases are expected to bring the level to . . . . 15 million by 1975." [4] Considering the school experience for the ordinary youngster who does not require highly individualized attention, one can be relatively optimistic about the next ten years. Because the school experience touches every child and hence every family, there has always been a reservoir of public interest in the school system which has been augmented by fear of Soviet competition. Fear plus construc-

[3] *Health, Education and Welfare Trends* (Washington, D.C.: U. S. Department of Health, Education, and Welfare, 1960), p. 26.

[4] *Young Workers under 18.*

tive interest will assure financial resources. Increasing salaries will ease somewhat the burden of the teacher shortage; while scientific advances in development of instructional aids will also help with this problem. The public eye on education has caused stirrings in the profession itself so that we begin to see an upgrading of teacher education and the widespread introduction of such methods as the four-track curriculum to develop the full potential of most children.[5]

Standing alongside the school services are those programs usually characterized as character-building and recreation. Here are included the Boy and Girl Scouts, the YM's and YW's, the boys' and girls' clubs, Campfire Girls, certain community centers, and the public recreational services. These organizations and programs have in varying degrees long enjoyed public confidence and support and can, at a minimum, at least look forward to expansion of service in proportion to expansion of population.[6]

Working together, the schools and the youth-serving agencies can, with relative ease, adapt their programs to the fact that they will serve more youngsters, and that most of these youngsters will live in the suburbs.[7] They can and will adapt themselves to the shifts in group composition resulting from the increasing mobility of population, as well as

[5] See John D. Koontz, "The Four Track Curriculum," *American Child,* XLIII, No. 2 (1961), 5–7.

[6] The omission of health services is deliberate since although special health facilities are urgently needed for adolescents, they are practically nonexistent except as related to, and incidental to, other services.

[7] Ralph M. Besse, *The Problems of Obsolescence in Urban Society,* address given at 1961 Annual Meeting of the Welfare Federation of Cleveland (Cleveland: Welfare Federation of Cleveland, 1961), p. 6.

to the tendency for more and more youths to receive more and more education before entering the labor market on a full-time basis.[8]

The schools and the youth-serving agencies can and will adapt themselves to social change as it bears upon most youths, but can they also serve the already damaged youngster who needs particular and specialized attention? The Conant Report speaks of 15 percent of our high school youngsters as academically superior.[9] While IQ does not insure freedom from emotional distress or behavioral problems, these youngsters are receiving increasing attention and tend to progress nicely through existing social institutions.[10] Robert J. Havinghurst estimates that in addition to the gifted 15 percent, some two thirds of our young people get along well under present educational and social conditions. Most graduate from high school and some go to college. "A quarter of this middle two-thirds, or 15 to 20 percent of the age group, do not graduate from high school, but they manage to get jobs at the age of 16 or 17, or to marry at those ages, and to grow up in a fairly competent manner." [11] Another 2 or 3 percent, according to Dr. Havinghurst, are physically handicapped or mentally retarded. "While it is next to impossible to provide opportunity [for these children] that will equate their chances for satisfactory growth to those enjoyed by 'normal' youngsters, society has made a determined effort in this direction." [12] Thanks, in large part, to the leadership given by parents of such disadvantaged children, it would appear, then, that the needs of 85 percent

[8] *Manpower—Challenge of the 1960's,* p. 15.

[9] Quoted in Robert J. Havinghurst, "A Statement of National Policy by the Commission on Youth and Work" (tentative draft prepared for Phi Delta Kappa), p. 2.

[10] *Ibid.* [11] *Ibid.* [12] *Ibid.,* p. 4.

of the youth population will be met in the next decade, at least to the extent that they are being met today. This will be accomplished by expanding the services in proportion to population growth. Note, however, that these services are not primarily social work services but may be subsumed under the rubric of "services for the general welfare" or social welfare services.

The remaining 15 percent of the youngsters require attention of a different order. They are youngsters whom Dr. Havinghurst characterizes as "alienated youth" [13] and whom I have characterized as "exiled." [14] These youngsters do not seem to accept the aspirations of the larger society. Their mode of life function is devalued by the larger community of which they are a part. They are unable to achieve full self-realization in a manner sanctioned by society. The roots of their difficulty are an intermixture of biological, social, and psychological factors with the predominant factors determining the symptom formation.

Where severe psychological deprivation is a basic element we may see psychopathy as the consequence, with its admixture of intrapersonal disorder and acting out. More frequently we see the psychological exile as manifesting what Dr. Laing calls "ontological insecurity." "The individual in the ordinary circumstances of living [who] may feel more unreal than real; in a literal sense, more dead than alive; precariously differentiated from the rest of the world, so that his identity and autonomy are always in question." [15]

[13] *Ibid.*

[14] Bertram M. Beck, "The Exile of Those in Conflict with the Law," *Casework Papers, 1955* (New York: Family Service Association of America, 1955), pp. 32–40.

[15] R. D. Laing, *The Divided Self* (Chicago: Quadrangle Books, 1960), p. 43.

Although the psychologically exiled exacts his primary toll from himself, society at large also pays, first through the loss of the contribution that the psychically wounded might have made and, secondly, through the need to handle the social problems engendered by mental illness, child neglect, marital incompatibility, and the like.

The exiles who suffer predominantly from social alienation exact a somewhat different toll from society. These are youngsters who, according to Cloward and Ohlin, use the delinquent gang to achieve satisfactions apparently denied them because of their position and status in the class structure:

> They are resentful because the equalitarian ideology of American society seems to promise them a fair share of the good things of life, and they realize that ethnic and class barriers will prevent them from attaining these goals. The feeling of unjust deprivation underlies alienation. . . . They seek support from others who are similarly alienated, and, with them they seek a collective solution to their common problem.[16]

The collective solution is, of course, the search for immediate gratification through unlawful means.

In this group of youngsters we find, of course, many of the school drop-outs. In 1959 there were about 616,000 out-of-school youth in the labor force. The size of this group is not expected to increase in the foreseeable future.[17] Amongst the sixteen-to-seventeen-year-old out-of-school youth there is about 20 percent unemployment.[18] Many of the socially exiled in the later adolescent years will be found in this

[16] Jackson Toby, review of Richard A. Cloward and Lloyd E. Ohlin, *Delinquency and Opportunity: a Theory of Delinquent Gangs* (Glencoe, Ill.: Free Press, 1960).

[17] *Young Workers under 18.* [18] *Ibid.*

"out-of-school-can't-find-a-job" group. Still others will be hanging on in school without any real engagement in the school program.

This 15 percent of exiled youngsters require special programs and services designed to restore to each of them identity and autonomy within a constructive relationship to the larger society. This task is today primarily that of the social work services rather than of the social welfare services. If, therefore, we are to maintain services for youth in 1970 at least to the extent that they are available in 1960, we must be able to demonstrate that the social work services too will at least grow in proportion to youth population. Unfortunately, this cannot be demonstrated.

The social work services—unlike the schools or the character-building agencies—are not now even beginning to meet today's need. Every practicing social worker knows that one can usually at least get an adolescent into the school program and one can usually find an organized group affiliation if it is needed; but try to find the professionally trained social worker who will actually engage himself in direct service to an adolescent. Just to hold the line of social work services for adolescents we have to increase services some 50 percent by 1975, and even if we do this, services will be as grossly inadequate as they are today.

Social work services demand professionally trained social workers. Preliminary findings of the Bureau of Labor Statistics Manpower Study, 1960, suggest that the ratio of professionally trained social workers to population has decreased in the past ten years and there is no reason to be optimistic about the next ten. Unless this trend can be reversed, accentuated personnel shortage will be one reason why we cannot even hold the line of service at today's inadequate level in 1970. Growing incidence of problem behavior may be another.

The social welfare services are faced merely with a tremendous growth in case load due to an expanding population. The social work services are probably faced with an increase in incidence of problems on top of the increase due to population expansion. The assumption is supported by statistics on the incidence of mental illness, juvenile delinquency, out-of-wedlock birth, and venereal disease. In each instance the over-all trend over the past decade is up, and there is no reason not to assume that the trend will continue upward for the next ten years.[19] Population trends, which portray the flight to the suburbs, the desolation of rural areas, and the deterioration of the inner city, suggest that more and more young people will tomorrow be living under conditions conducive to social and psychological exile.

Looking ahead, then, it can be predicted that the alienated 15 percent who require social work services today will by 1970 have grown to a proportion closer to 25 or 30 percent. When this occurs our schools and general youth-serving organizations geared to meet the needs of normal rather than social or psychologically deviant youth will find it increasingly difficult to function. Obviously, we need at this point to give attention to necessary modifications of our social institutions so that we effectively incorporate into the living community 100 percent of these youngsters rather than 85 percent.

Part of our problem in effectively serving and hence reincorporating the dissident 15 percent in the past has been the illusion that by working with the most domesticated,

[19] *Health, Education and Welfare Trends,* pp. 10, 43, 47, 85.

conforming, easy-to-reach, the number of less conforming, hard-to-reach would somehow diminish. This is the myth of prevention which mistakenly applies a concept suitable to public health to social welfare where it is wholly inapplicable. We can inoculate a healthy man against smallpox and predict accurately that he will not get the disease. We have saved him and ourselves a bad time. Unfortunately, nobody can tell us what we can do with a healthy young child that will enable us accurately to predict that as a consequence of our action that child will not join the exiled when he becomes an adolescent.

Despite this inability systematically to prevent, school systems exclude the deviant supposedly in the interests of the larger number of healthy children. For the most part, the large youth-serving organizations are not geared for the exiled youngster. In the offices of the social work agencies which have as their acknowledged responsibility the treatment of the alienated group, one rarely finds the adolescent. More often, one finds the adult or the younger child and the myth of prevention—the unspoken hope that if we work with everyone except the one who most needs our attention the problem will solve itself. The adolescent is most frequently seen by the court social worker or the social worker in the mental hospital when behavior has forced attention. The attendance officer also sees the adolescent in the flesh, but not so the school social worker. He is most often attached to the elementary grades, doing this so-called "preventive" job.

I submit that to address ourselves to a problem we must name it and work with it. In the present instance it is the problem of alienated youth. To develop a social strategy for the solution of this problem there must be an analysis of its social, cultural, economic, and psychological roots. From such an analysis must spring a plan of management, and we may be surprised to find that we have been in error in viewing social work services as the major means of dealing with the reincorporation of alienated youth.

Instead, we may find ourselves advocating the launching on a nationwide scale of prototypes of New York City's Higher Horizon program. This is an educational program designed "to identify, encourage and stimulate children from low socio-economic, culturally deprived areas to raise their educational and vocational sights, even as high as college for the more able." This project was launched in Junior High School 43 in 1956. A study made of that school's graduates prior to the launching of the project showed that 60 percent dropped out before graduating from senior high school and less than 4 percent went on to liberal arts colleges. These were typically socially exiled youngsters who did not view themselves as learners who could climb the ladder of the American dream. The basic task of the Higher Horizons program was to alter the youngster's image of society and himself. The success in accomplishing this is evident in the fact that instead of 60 percent drop-outs in the first project class, 64 percent gained senior high school diplomas. Thirty-four percent went on to some kind of post high school education! [20]

I am not, of course, advocating this one program as the answer to reincorporation of the exiled. Equally worthy of attention is a somewhat similar program in the Chicago schools with a broader community base.[21] Also abroad is a

[20] Daniel Schrieber, "Higher Horizons," *American Child,* XLIII, No. 1 (1961), 12.

[21] Arnita Boswell, "Coordinating Community Forces for Development of the Potentials of Children and Youth," paper presented at the National Conference on Social Welfare, 1961; mimeographed.

concept of a publically guaranteed work experience for those who leave school between the ages of sixteen and nineteen. These plans envision various work-training opportunities provided by government-industry-labor cooperation, particularly for the school drop-out who cannot be absorbed in industry.[22]

My point is not that social work must find the answer in any one of the programs named, but that it must seek the answer by evolving a social strategy based on an understanding of the roots of social alienation. Such a strategy must be designed to counteract the forces of racial, social, psychological, and economic discrimination that push young people out of the aspirations of the larger society.

We must begin to think in terms of social problems and see individual problems within that framework. We need to beware the tendency to see the answer to every social problem in the aspect of practice most familiar to us. From this myopic point of view comes our tendency to think that all the world's problems would be solved if only we had more and more caseworkers to help more and more people.

My objection is not to casework or group work, as such—far from it. I have such deep and abiding respect for the helping potential of social work methods that I would like to see the short supply husbanded and actually available as part of a total social policy—not as a substitute for social policy. I would like to see us use our social policy skills for planning and our community organization methods to involve welfare services and social work services in getting the plan off the ground. Once launched, it is the refocused programs in schools and youth-serving organizations which would handle the problem of social alienation en masse. Social work services become adjunctive to these broader

[22] Havinghurst, *op. cit.*, pp. 12–19.

programs, enabling them to function by giving particularized attention where needed.

To accomplish such an end requires a degree of social planning today unknown. One of the major obstacles to such an achievement is our own vested interest in our own island of service. Each agency, and now even individual social workers, develops a particular clientele without regard to any overview of social need. To deploy our professional resources in the public interest is the challenge that confronts us. If we fail, there is reason to believe that by 1970 our agencies and allied social institutions will break down under the impact of the ever-growing number of exiled individuals. If we succeed, it will be because under the lash of our troubled times we will have finally achieved our glorious potential as a profession. I believe we will succeed.

EXPERIMENTAL APPROACHES IN DEPRIVED AREAS

by Arthur Hillman

SEVERAL LINES OF DEVELOPMENT in thought and practice have converged to stimulate experimentation[1] in service programs in poorer areas of large cities. The implications of the Bradley Buell study[2] in St. Paul have received attention in many places, and there is new interest in aggressive work with chronic problem families. Special demonstration programs in family service are parallel with, and sometimes related to, work that reaches out to individuals and youth groups in conflict situations—those prone to delinquency. Trying out new programs is part of a widespread movement within neighborhood centers, in keeping with traditional settlement house emphases on the family and neighborhood, which in recent years has reflected a more deliberate concern about establishing priorities in services and adapting to changing local conditions.[3]

New forms of collaboration between public and volun-

[1] "Experimentation" is used partly in the popular sense of trying something new or doing something tentatively. However, many of the programs include concurrent work in evaluating results, and some are based on scientific research designs.

[2] Bradley Buell and Associates, *Community Planning for Human Services* (New York: Columbia University Press, 1952).

[3] *Neighborhood Centers Today* (New York: National Federation of Settlements and Neighborhood Centers, 1960), Chaps. II and III.

tary agencies have developed in several cities, notably in connection with services in public housing projects. The latter, especially those with large concentrations of low-income residents, tend to get a residual group of multi-problem families who are visibly in need of special service. The planning and provision of appropriate services in public housing are increasingly accepted as community responsibilities.

The public schools in our major cities have faced the educational problems that arise from transiency, congested housing, and the lack of encouragement to academic achievement found in "culturally deprived" [4] neighborhoods. The presence of over-age children in elementary schools and the large number of teen-age drop-outs have pointed up the need for in-school programs aimed at instilling in the children the motivation to continue their education. Such programs are being undertaken along with new attempts to reach out to parents and local institutions. In some ways, this movement is a renaissance of the community school idea.[5] Churches have also been concerned with the effects of mobility and population change on their parishes and are broadening their concepts of evangelism and social service.[6] In some places, they are addressing

[4] The descriptive term "culturally deprived" should not be taken to signify that lower-class areas do not have cultures which may be stable and complex.

[5] Fourteen "great cities" are associated in the planning and review of local projects dealing with school organization, curriculum, and community relationships. This program has substantial Ford Foundation support and is under the national leadership of Dr. Benjamin C. Willis, General Superintendent of Schools, Chicago.

[6] *The City Church,* bimonthly periodical, National Council of the Churches of Christ in the U.S.A., New York; Walter Kloetzli, *The City Church—Death or Renewal* (Philadelphia: Muhlenberg Press,

themselves to the task of strengthening local community life and particularly to the dearth of indigenous leadership for social action.

These developments are often accompanied by new efforts in research, especially efforts to evaluate the results of demonstration programs. The theoretical background of research has included notably the growing interest among sociologists in the study of social class and, in particular, a new sophistication about subcultures within the lower class as they help explain delinquency patterns, resistance to change, and the whole problem of motivation.[7] Such refinements of thought have delineated environmental factors more clearly and have suggested fruitful lines for further research.

Services to people with problems include concurrent and related work with families and individuals, help to existing groups, and efforts to create new social structures within neighborhoods. Extensions of the generic approach of neighborhood centers to public housing projects are numerous throughout the country. The problems involved in creating a new social milieu to match the newness of physical surroundings are often acute because of the absence of any neighborhood organization on which to build. Moreover, the general expectations of the tenants are often fearful or at least conducive to isolation.

One example of a many-pronged approach is found at the

1961); Dennis Clark, *The Crises in Our Cities* (New York: Sheed and Ward, 1959).

[7] *Neighborhood Centers Today,* Chap. III; Richard A. Cloward and Lloyd Ohlin, *Delinquency and Opportunity: a Theory of Delinquent Gangs* (Glencoe, Ill.: Free Press, 1960); Oliver Moles and others, *A Selective Review of Research and Theory on Delinquency* (Ann Arbor, Mich.: Survey Research Center, University of Michigan, 1959).

South End Housing Project in Boston where a cooperative venture is being carried on by the United South End Settlements and the Boston Housing Authority. It came about as the result of their mutual concerns about problems in the housing project, such as the increasing concentration of multiproblem families, vandalism, and the behavior of youth, both those in the project and outsiders. United South End Settlements directs the program and provides two trained social workers, one with a background in community organization and the other a group worker experienced in work with hard-to-reach youth. The Housing Authority employs a full-time trained social worker and has made available a centrally located six-room apartment which serves as headquarters for the program.

The program, which combines casework, group work, and community organization skills, is directed to the entire housing project community. The goals are to reduce interethnic and other tensions, to make maximum use of community resources, to help with homemaking skills and adjustments to project living, to deal constructively with delinquent behavior, and to improve the channels of communication between residents and project management. Here, as elsewhere, there is need to develop a sense of community pride and positive identification among tenants in relation to the project. Attention is also given to relations between tenants and the neighborhood.

In New York, Henry Street Settlement conducts a program within the nearby LaGuardia Houses, a large public housing project. Here almost eleven hundred families, some five thousand persons, strangers to each other, moved into nine sixteen-story buildings. There was a mixture of ethnic backgrounds, with Puerto Ricans, Negroes, and Jews predominating.

Lack of identification with their new community is an important factor in the newcomers' lack of concern for the proper care of the new facilities and equipment. . . . Group work and recreation services had been carried on in the community center, which occupies the two lower floors of one of the LaGuardia buildings. The Henry Street Settlement operates this center under a plan of public and private agency cooperation whereby the New York City Housing Authority provides equipment and maintenance service, and . . . assigns a recreation worker to private agencies who are responsible for the program. Group activities, however, proved inadequate in creating the needed sense of community among the residents. . . . A more aggressive approach seemed to be needed.[8]

The "aggressive approach" was implemented by home visits, first by social work students and later by professional staff, and by various informal contacts designed to acquaint the residents with available community services. Most noteworthy have been the floor meetings, arranged by the home visitors as the first steps toward better understanding among neighbors and toward tenant organization. The visitors have learned, in the course of their work, about overcoming hostilities by patience and persistence; about cultural patterns, such as those of the Puerto Ricans who were courteous but not necessarily responsive; and about the emergence of leadership, with the emphasis on stimulating self-help. The local residents have begun to experience success in small projects and to plan for new services, such as a cooperative nursery school.

Intensive work with families is illustrated by the Hard Core project of Hudson Guild Neighborhood House, in New York, which is surrounded by the John Elliott Housing Project. The neighborhood center and the housing manage-

[8] *Neighborhood Centers Today,* pp. 32–37; Murray E. Ortof, "Public Housing: New Neighbors in Old Communities," *Social Work,* IV, No. 2 (1959), 33.

ment have worked together on numerous projects, but this one is focused on those "troubled and troublesome families" who face the threat of eviction because of their behavior:

The Hudson Guild Counseling Service (the psychiatric clinic) assumed direction of the Guild's coordinated effort to help these families. Diagnostic studies by the clinic team formed the basis of treatment plans and gave some clues to aspects of personality that blocked these clients' constructive use of community resources. The studies also enabled the staff to interpret these clients' needs, strengths, and limitations to the many people who should be involved in helping them: the Housing manager, the Guild administration, group workers, camp registrar, day care counselor, nursery teachers, and others.[9]

As a result of intensive work, the need for evictions has been minimized. According to a recent report:

Six families are no longer described as "undesirable tenants" by Housing management. In no case, however, does the staff feel that sufficient improvement has been achieved to warrant closing the case in the immediate future. Providing long-term supportive treatment for these families may well be an economically justifiable use of community resources.

The factors contributing to the success of the project seem to be: the bi-monthly conference with the Housing Authority staff, resulting in an integrated and individualized approach for each family; treatment based on an intensive psychosocial diagnostic study by the clinic team and carried out in a neighborhood house already known to and used by the families concerned; and the effective utilization of other services of Hudson Guild (day care, day camp) because of close cooperation between the Counseling Service and staff in other departments.[10]

Experimental approaches in deprived areas have thus included teamwork between different parts of multiservice agencies and notably new forms of coordination of services

[9] *Neighborhood Centers Today,* p. 190. [10] *Ibid.,* p. 191.

between agencies. An interesting example is that of group work services provided to youngsters referred by the schools because of behavior problems. The Detroit School–Community Behavior Project was organized and is directed by the schools. The Neighborhood Service Organization recognizes the procedures and autonomy of each school in its cooperation. The goals are in terms of improvement for each child in school achievement and group relationships.

Since the school classroom is an ideal setting in which to detect possible symptoms of emotional disturbance in a given child, the teachers in the project schools are provided with a checklist which notes forty danger signs. Should the teacher feel that the child in question needs help, he is referred to the school Action Team. The behavior problem is then discussed by competent and experienced officials of the school, the visiting teacher, his regular teachers, the consulting psychiatrist, the school nurse, and a representative from NSO. From these monthly meetings comes the plan of action for the children in need of aid. If the child needs individual tutoring or specific health services, for example, the Action Team will arrange for help from cooperating agencies.

If after-school group activity is likely to be helpful, NSO provides it on referral by the school Action Team. NSO now has a relationship with eight schools in this program. The services it furnishes are much like any other group work. The NSO worker meets youngsters after school and may take them by car or bus to various places for diversified activities. Such trips, however, are more than play periods or tours or projects to supplement the school program. The worker's professional observations of the child in these small groups are reported back to the Action Team for planning further treatment in relation to the behavior problems evident. Moreover, the NSO worker may make home visits to gain an understanding of the parents' view of the problem, perhaps before the Action Team has made its full diagnosis. Talks with the youngsters themselves also are revealing and help them to understand why they have been referred to the group for special attention.

The quality of teamwork within the school, and between it and the community, varies with the local leadership, but principals and others are gaining new insights and skills from the experience with Action Teams. NSO staff members recognize too that they have much to learn with respect to services to such referral groups.[11]

The Higher Horizons Project in New York City has received national attention. It is designed to enrich the total educational experience of children whose backgrounds are limited culturally. It is a community-based program and includes cooperation of agencies such as Manhattanville Community Centers. The casework department there has received referrals from the nearby school and cooperative planning has been carried on between the school personnel and the agency's group work staff, resulting in work with parents and special remedial or tutorial work at the Center.[12]

Operation Poplar, a Philadelphia interagency program, was started in 1957 and is scheduled to end in May, 1961. It has proceeded on the theory that family breakdown and delinquency are products of general social disorganization in poor areas characterized by economically impoverished people, bad housing, contradictory adult standards of behavior, and weak social controls. The objective has been to build local leadership and family strength so that delinquency would not have a favorable climate, and to improve the whole framework of social relationships rather

[11] *Ibid.*, pp. 200–201. NSO *Newsletter,* December, 1958, p. 2.

[12] "A Report of the Role of Manhattanville Community Centers, Inc. in the 'Higher Horizons' Program at P.S. 125, 1959–60" (New York: Manhattanville Community Centers, Inc., 1960; mimeographed); Martin Mayer, "The Good Slum Schools," *Harper's,* May, 1961, pp. 46–52.

than attempt to work on delinquency directly as symptomatic behavior.

The core staff of Operation Poplar consists of a director, a counseling worker for individuals and families, an area youth worker for boys, and a community organizer. Every effort is made to involve neighborhood adults in volunteer work, however simple, and to organize neighborhood and tenant councils. Another emphasis in the program has been the case conference approach, which includes not only the several cooperating agencies represented on the Operation Poplar staff, but also teachers, housing officials, probation officers, and others who may be directly related to a particular case. One agency is assigned responsibility for following through to make sure that treatment plans are coordinated and made effective.[13]

An aggressive approach in work with families, as well as new cooperation between public and voluntary agencies, is well illustrated in a program started in 1956 at Baden Street Settlement, Rochester, New York. Its most distinct contribution is the resourceful use of volunteers who are given special training and work under professional direction. Volunteers report that they have gained not only personal satisfactions but also new insight into lower-class family life problems.

This year forty-four volunteer case aides provided direct service to forty-two multiproblem families. The volunteers do regular visiting of clients who may have come to the casework department through another part of the settlement program or have been referred by the relocation office, public assistance, or other agencies. Case aides channel their

[13] *Neighborhood Centers Today,* pp. 120–24.

referrals through the professional staff of the settlement.[14] Their supportive role and their specific services unquestionably extend the effectiveness of professional staff in the time-consuming work with problem families.

Neighborhood centers often include in their varied programs some services to individuals and families, typically those growing out of group work or neighborhood contacts. This may mean referral based on informally acquired knowledge of the person's needs or may extend to intensive casework by a specialist on the center staff. The pooling of knowledge about a problem family by several members of the staff is fairly common procedure.

A special demonstration of integrated services within a neighborhood agency setting—Huntington Family Centers in Syracuse, New York—is noteworthy in several respects. There is a controlled intake and treatment load. Group workers and nursery school teachers who see children twice a week or more, family counselors who meet with mothers in groups, and caseworkers who see some families regularly and others frequently during crisis periods share their knowledge of families through regular conferences. Psychiatric consultation is a weekly part of the skilled diagnosis and planning of treatment. Interagency conferences are an important tool in the helping process. There are mothers' groups and parent education classes. A special effort is made to reach fathers through camp activity or family nights at the center. The Trading Post, a clothing exchange, gives the agency staff a chance for contact with families in need of con-

[14] *Ibid.*, pp. 87–92; reports from Baden Street Settlement, Rochester, including "Reaching Out to Hard-to-Reach, Multi-Problem Families through the Use of Volunteer Case Aides," March, 1961, and "Patterns of Change in Families Assigned to the Volunteer Case Aide Program, April 1, 1958–January 31, 1960."

centrated services and is part of an aggressive approach acceptable to clients.[15]

The Huntington Family Centers experience indicates that the accessibility of services located in a neighborhood center is an important feature. Moreover, there may well be a positive orientation to the agency because the nearby people come there voluntarily and informally for other activities. This is the rationale back of a project in Vancouver, British Columbia, where the Family Service Society assigned a worker to each of two neighborhood houses for two days a week. The experiment covered a twenty-seven-month period ending in December, 1957. After an evaluation of the project, the services became a part of the regular program of the two houses in 1958:

> Emphasis was placed on work with incipient problems, although service was also given to multi-problem families. Problems were identified at the time of initial contact, or registration for participation in group activities, and through the observed behavior of children in the program. There were also voluntary requests for service from House members, sometimes on behalf of others in the community.[16]

[15] *Neighborhood Centers Today,* pp. 75–80. "Multi-Service Project for Troubled Families in a Social Settlement Center in Syracuse, New York," July, 1960; a three-year report, to June, 1961, is to be published.

[16] *Neighborhood Centers Today,* p. 71. "The latest development here in relation to the Joint Family Service 'approach' is that the Chest and Councils Research Department, headed by Dr. Joseph Lagey and with him Miss Beverly Ayres as research assistant, both formerly with the Family Centered Project of St. Paul, is preparing to conduct a research study of the effects of use of the method in working with 'multi-problem' families in the Alexandra House neighbourhood, and possibly in the Gordon House neighbourhood, in Vancouver. Plans are to have a 'control group' and to do a thoroughly scientific evaluation. This should prove whether or not the method is an improvement." Letter from G. A. Whiten, Executive Director, Alexandra Neighbourhood House, Vancouver, B.C., May 3, 1961.

Thinking in local community terms, we find that self-help is a keynote in a number of interesting service approaches.[17] The Self-Help Housing program sponsored by Friends Neighborhood Guild in Philadelphia deserves to be well known. In South Philadelphia, staff work by United Neighbors Association has been directed toward citizen participation in short-term projects with rather specific objectives. The goal is to develop such leadership that the agency service can be withdrawn and the group continue on its own. Obviously, however, there is an element of gamble involved in the timing of withdrawing professional help.

The self-help theme is well illustrated in Houston in the work of Neighborhood Centers Association, much of which is done in suburbs or in newer areas of the city. These are not comparable to the inner city with its ingrown forms of deprivation, but there are needs for recreation services which local residents have been organized to help provide or to sponsor.

The emphasis on helping people to help themselves obviously ties in with methods of social action, or political competence in a broad sense. This may include special efforts at leadership training such as a course for public housing tenants given by the East Harlem Project in New York City. The content covered information about community services, methods of fact finding, types of leadership and problems of communication.

Although participants in the East Harlem course were interested in having a better community, some of them did not want to be called leaders.[18] This reluctance of capable

[17] *Neighborhood Centers Today,* Chap. I, includes case studies of the programs mentioned in this and the next paragraph.

[18] Leonard Brickman, "Finding Leadership in a Low-Income Urban Area," *Adult Leadership,* IX (1961), 273–74, 294.

people to let themselves be labeled as "leaders" is understandable because they do not want to seem pretentious or to be grasping for power. Among Puerto Ricans particularly there is some tendency to avoid letting oneself be set apart from the group. However, there is a need for people, especially newcomers to the city, to acquire basic community information and to learn some simple skills in conducting meetings. Therefore, such training has its place and would supplement rather than supplant the finding of "real" leaders in the process of working on specific projects or local programs.

As we look at these many examples, we may ask: What are the principles or policies which are being tested more or less experimentally? What is being learned which gives new content to the currently popular term "community development"?

1. The various special programs provide a fresh look at whole problems with many facets rather than at categories of services. The approach is situational rather than a matter of deciding whether certain problems lend themselves to the use of specialized skills.

2. A new awareness of the importance of the *relationship* between professional workers and clients—the steadiness and strength of relationship—is emerging. This is an old-fashioned concept, with idealistic or spiritual overtones, but it is proving to be professionally reputable and practical.

There is a danger that special, experimental, short-term project demonstrations will be cut off when funds are exhausted, even if the results would justify continuation. The families or neighborhoods being served may be left with new feelings of deprivation or rejection. This danger is clearly evident also in work with problem groups, such as street gangs. Special attention should be given to all that is involved in the termination of the services of a special youth worker who may be more needed by another group in a continuing program.

We should recognize too that there are subleties of personal growth involved in a process of social interaction. We must be on guard against assuming that everything that is worth doing can be measured quantitatively. Some growth in personal strength and capacity for interpersonal relationships may be marginal to those aspects which can be measured, and the evaluation of some growth may best be made, if at all, only years after the conclusion of a project.

3. The goals of projects such as those described, as well as of work with delinquent gangs,[19] include not only individual or family "movement" but also changes in standards of groups and of the culture of a neighborhood. The sociological orientation of many local programs has made for a departure from the individualistic, escapist criterion of successful readjustment toward more thought of changes in neighborhood values, with reference to education, conforming behavior, and living standards generally. The inclusion of research evaluations in many projects has had the practical effect of requiring a statement of specific goals, in realistic terms. Part of the reality which is being worked with is the subcultural material, and from knowledge of this sturdy stuff comes the recognition that individuals or families are bound up with habits and allegiances which often have to be dealt with collectively.

4. With the focus on local areas or neighborhoods, there needs to be a strong sense of the reciprocal relationship between the parts and the whole in a metropolitan commu-

[19] *Neighborhood Centers Today,* Chap. III.

nity. There may be a romantic enchantment with the social life of a locality, but we also know that public policies in the municipality or nation and the quality of city and metropolitan planning all have their impact, good or bad, on an area. Both governmental and economic decisions made at a distance may profoundly influence local communities.[20]

Eventually, the development of strength within a local community may affect the tone of city politics; for most cities, however, the reverse is true: the present climate of over-all leadership is most relevant to what happens locally. Beyond the metropolitan scene, we know well—but need to emphasize—that legislation on public housing, social security, minimum wages, job retraining, and the like, are all important to the strength and stability of families and neighborhoods. The more experience we have with experimental approaches to deprived areas, the better may be the local methodology, and the more informed may be the local basis for necessary large-scale remedies.

[20] Roland L. Warren, "Toward a Reformulation of Community Theory," *Human Organization,* XV, No. 2 (1956), 8–11.

THE SOCIAL WORKER IN INTERGROUP RELATIONS

by Antonia Pantoja

THE WORLD AROUND US—near and far—vibrates with the profound and eloquent efforts of Africans, Asians, Hispanic Americans and North Americans who are seeking identification, self-determination, and fair and equal opportunities. These are movements characterized by courage, freshness of approach, and the youthfulness of new leaders. Although many of the struggles outside the United States have political or nationalistic motivation, they all share a similar spirit. The movements in the United States have the stamp of courage expressed by Martin Luther King, when he reminded white Americans that the Negro will win in his struggle because he will endure pain and injustice in the measure that the white man can inflict them. These movements have the force of dedication which creates new techniques and new leaders. The oppressed and depressed peoples of the world look to these new leaders for guidance in their struggle for a share of the education, richness, and comforts of life; but more than that, they demand the dignity that should accompany man's relationship to life.

In the United States, during the sixties, we will witness vast population changes in our metropolitan areas. "New neighbors" will continue to migrate to industrial centers as our economy expands to meet the challenges that face our country. The American Negro's fight for equal opportunity in the South will result in growing economic and physical harassment, causing many to flock to more liberal climates in the North. Despite severe handicaps, our minority groups are climbing the ladder of economic success and seeking adequate housing in hitherto all-white neighborhoods. Extensive urban renewal projects will disperse large numbers of the less privileged groups throughout our cities. Tight housing markets will slow down the white exodus to suburbia. Aggressive social action programs being implemented by leaders of minority groups will have a growing impact upon urban living. Are we prepared to cope with the intergroup problems created by these powerful social forces?

The human revolution taking place in this country as well as throughout the world will bring new relationships among groups, but in the process of accommodation there will be conflict and disorder. Can the profession of social work, and group workers in particular, contribute to the establishment of positive new relationships? Social work has long recognized these human problems and the need for their solutions. In the year 1949 we were saying:

> In a long evolutionary struggle the welfare premise gradually coming to be accepted is that the basic human needs of all children, of all persons, irrespective of class and caste, of nation and race, should be met, not ignored or frustrated; and that exploitation, ruthless competition, and armed aggression, as ways of satisfying one's own needs at the expense of others, are inadmissible.[1]

A young and dynamic profession still in the process of crystallizing has a chance to make an outstanding and last-

[1] Gordon Hamilton, "Helping People—the Growth of a Profession,"

ing contribution to intergroup relations at this very crucial moment in its history. The ethical and philosophical commitment of social workers should make it possible for them to become good intergroup relations practitioners. We are faced with a great need to help our fellow men find the democratic ways to change the social, political, and economic factors which deprive them of their rights:

> More and more it appears that social work is essential at that point in the interaction between the individual and his social environment where, either through limitations within the individual or because of his situation and the nature of his environment, effective functioning is hampered or has broken down.[2]

The traditional employment of group workers in settlements, community centers, and other agencies that offer leisure-time services has been a legitimate use of our skills and knowledge. The same can be said about our success in bringing our services into settings like mental hospitals, correctional institutions, and children's institutions, but not enough social workers are involved in intergroup relations. Intergroup relations is not only a legitimate field where we can contribute our skills, but it is a field where a group worker is one of the best equipped professionals to function adequately.

I have chosen three examples from activities typical of the work of the New York City Commission on Intergroup Relations. They will help to prove my point that group work is the profession which can bring to such situations the

---

in *Social Work as Human Relations* (New York: Columbia University Press, 1949), p. 4.

[2] Werner W. Boehm, *Objectives of the Social Work Curriculum of the Future,* The Comprehensive Report of the Curriculum Study, Vol. I (New York: Council on Social Work Education, Inc., 1959), p. 50.

best skills and knowledge and the commitment that is necessary to function successfully and adequately in these and in similar situations.

1. *Community tension in relation to school integration.*—We are all familiar with the *de facto* segregation of a large number of the public schools in New York City. As part of one of the methods used to desegregate the school system during the early summer of 1959, the Board of Education decided to transfer about 365 Negro and Puerto Rican children from schools in the Bedford-Stuyvesant neighborhoods into Queens. The Queens communities have an all-white population of homeowners of long residence in the area. Although the Board of Education did not announce this move as an integration measure, the parents in Glendale and Ridgewood realized that integration was the real reason for the shift, rather than an effort to utilize better school facilities.

This situation brought about a series of disturbances carried on by Queens parents who tried to oppose the transfer of the Brooklyn children into their schools. The group which took the matter into their hands was the Glendale Taxpayers Association, composed of many local Parent-Teacher Association members and officers. Disorderly elements from the organized bigoted groups came to the area to aggravate the tension. During the summer months a job had to be done to check the negative activities, to mobilize the forces of good will, and to insure that when the children entered the schools in September, no violence would occur.

The group workers who were involved in this crisis functioned in several different roles:

a) As professionals representing an official city agency, they attended meetings of the opposing group to help tone down actions so that the group would act only within the law.

b) As technicians and educators, they assembled the facts, reached groups within and outside the community, and helped them to disseminate these facts to check the rumors being spread by others.

c) As enablers, liaisons, and mediators, they called a series of meetings with the clergy in the area, with heads of organizations, with the main intergroup relations agencies of the city, with the community leaders in Bedford-Stuyvesant and in Glendale-Ridgewood. At these meetings the different groups and agencies were helped to devise programs of action.

d) As liaison between the community and the Board of Education, they planned and conducted various meetings between the parents and the principals, teachers, and officials of the Board of Education.

e) As program experts and planners, they prepared a network of services covering the first few weeks of school, in order to prevent any violence to the children, to allay the fears of the parents who were sending their children to the Queens schools, and to help foresee any problems that would be created in the schools by this situation. These programs were all performed by volunteers, community groups, and churches.

2. *ASPIRA: the creation of a new agency.*—One of the most important tasks in bringing about sound intergroup relations is that of helping the minority to develop its own resources, its own leadership. The measure of the success attained by minority groups is achieving their due place in society is directly related to the quality of their leadership.

The Commission on Intergroup Relations has various programs directed to this need.

ASPIRA, a project designed to develop new leadership in the Puerto Rican community of New York through the creation of a new agency, provides my second example of the efficacy of the group worker in intergroup relations.

A group worker originated the idea of ASPIRA. The worker offered a new concept: the training of leadership in disadvantaged or minority groups must include the motivation and guidance of those members of the groups who possess the ability and talents to enter professional, technical, and artistic fields. This is necessary in order to create a pool of persons who can function on a par with the rest of the population, give leadership to their group, and place it on an equal basis with the organizations and leadership of the majority groups.

As an organizer, the worker has brought together a board of directors to administer the project. The worker has also played the role of technical advisor to the chairman of the board and other officers to secure from foundations the funds necessary to sustain and fully develop the project. (ASPIRA has received two grants from two foundations.)

When it opens its doors for service ASPIRA will be a private agency, staffed primarily by Puerto Rican professionals, with a Puerto Rican board of directors. It will represent a self-help effort. It will be in itself a symbol of its own purposes.

3. *The neighborhood clinic.*—My last example is that of a service offered by the Community Relations Division of the Commission on Intergroup Relations.

The neighborhood clinic offers consultative services and

guidance to groups from neighborhoods that are having intergroup problems. In cases where the group does not have the appropriate structure to work with the problems faced, the worker can help them to organize an intergroup relations committee. The worker will enable the group to identify and diagnose the problems that beset their area and will help them to secure the necessary facts and materials, including a survey of existing resources that they could use.

The worker helps the group to devise a practicable plan of action to solve or alleviate their problems. As an expert, he brings in program aids and makes referrals to other agencies. Using the prestige of his agency, the worker helps the citizens' group to take their problems to the proper city agencies and officials.

These are not the only programs which the Commission offers, but they indicate the kinds of problems with which people need help if they are to find answers and solutions.

When the relationship among groups breaks down, the Commission staff find themselves propelled into dealing with tension and violence in local neighborhoods. We also engage, at the top levels of governmental and private agencies, in negotiations that will change, create, or modify policies and administrative decisions that affect minorities. We train minority leadership in the fields that govern their fate and progress, and we train "majority" leadership in techniques and programs that will help their own groups learn how to live with people who are different. We work with neighborhood organizations to help integrate newcomers into homogeneous neighborhoods, to prevent changing neighborhoods from becoming ghettos, to involve the minority leadership in the decision-making structures, and to handle local incidents of prejudice and bigotry.

Is there a place in this kind of work for more group workers? Have we as a profession done all we could in our work with adults and young adults? Is there a need for other than recreational programs for adults?

Many group work agencies do not service adults at all, or have very weak adult divisions. Those who have adult divisions usually do not offer programs that can help adults to solve the problems of urban living. Minority citizens are anxious to find solutions to the problems of the education of their children and of housing conditions, to their problems in relating to governmental structures and in receiving necessary city services. They want solutions to problems that arise from the rapid movement and change going on in their very block and neighborhood. These are the issues of intergroup relations, and these are the programs to which we as social workers have to address ourselves to if we want to serve people in the world of today.

INTERGROUP RELATIONS AND COMMUNITY WELFARE PLANNING

by George W. Culberson

THE SOCIAL WORK PROFESSION, based upon a belief in the dignity of all men, was characterized in the past by courageous fighting against social injustice. In 1960, Whitney M. Young, Jr., took "full swing" at the hesitancy and temerity of persons in the social work field when it came to discussion or action involving race relations.[1] He went on to show that all too many agencies reflect the community mores and patterns in regard to board membership, employment of staff, and service to clients or membership. To summarize his conclusions: Whitney Young believes that many social workers try not to offend, have avoided controversy, and have become as class-conscious as those they serve. To this I add the following thought: the movement toward more and more use of the united fund, with the resulting involvement of the community power structure in this effort, has increased the probability that social workers and agencies will avoid identification with the problems of intergroup relations.

[1] Whitney M. Young, Jr., "Intergroup Relations and Social Work Practice," in *The Social Welfare Forum, 1960* (New York: Columbia University Press, 1960), pp. 146–53.

The National Association of Intergroup Relations Officials (NAIRO) has developed outside the framework of the social work field, and the membership has a relatively small percentage of social workers. It could very well be that the existence of NAIRO is due largely to the fact that the social work profession is no longer in the forefront in fighting against social injustice generally, and against racial and ethnic injustice particularly.

"Intergroup relations" may be defined in various ways. In its broadest sense, it is the generic term covering interracial relations, interreligious relations, and interethnic relations. It encompasses civil rights problems of Negroes, Jews, Orientals, Puerto Ricans, Mexican Americans, and others who experience discrimination or segregation; cultural problems faced by American Indians, Southern mountain whites, and others who are transplanted abruptly from rural to urban living; and interreligious tensions arising out of Church-State issues. At least peripherally, it includes the problems of the foreign-born and of migrant farm laborers, the problems springing from denial of civil liberties, and the problems of the aged in the area of employment discrimination.

Practitioners in the field of intergroup relations are concerned with elimination of discriminatory practices which prevent an individual, because of his group identification, from moving about in a free society and achieving his full potential as an American citizen. The major areas of concern are basic and include equality of opportunity in employment, housing, education, and places of public accommodation. It is recognized at once that these concerns have likewise been the traditional concerns of those in the social work profession. The causes for which Jane Addams fought included problems of immigration, woman suffrage, recognition of labor unions, an end to child labor, regulation of working hours, and the like.

Intergroup relations is, finally, a field of occupation for more than fifteen hundred full-time workers employed by governmental and private intergroup relations agencies throughout the United States. These agencies maintain 600 offices in at least 150 cities in 43 states. Intergroup practitioners possess a unique blend of skills and knowledge. From a variety of disciplines they have drawn and adapted techniques of community organization, social action, education, investigation and enforcement, and conciliation and mediation. Around these has developed a body of knowledge that incorporates both the research findings of the social sciences and the rich experience of this emerging field.

It has always seemed to me that there is an unnatural separation between social work and intergroup relations. Both the goals and the methods are not only compatible but identical. Alexander J. Allen expresses the same idea in these words:

> I would like to venture the thought that had social work developed a little faster in the late thirties and early forties, particularly in the field of community organization, or had the problems of interracial relationships developed more slowly during that period, there would now be no doubt but that the field we describe as intergroup relations is a proper part of the field of social work.[2]

Agencies now considered to be intergroup relations agencies had their beginning as agencies to foster and promote group welfare and developed during the period of large-scale immigration in the closing decades of the last century.

[2] Alexander J. Allen, "Professionalization of Intergroup Relations Work and Workers," *Journal of Intergroup Relations,* I, No. 2 (1960), 41.

By and large, they were sponsored by religious organizations. Their activities were almost entirely group centered but had as their purpose hastening the admission of the immigrant group into the main stream of American life. Arnold Aronson, in discussing this point, says:

> The pattern of church organization at the time was not only along denominational lines but along ethnic lines within the several denominations. . . . The present pattern of social welfare institutions along sectarian lines derives largely from this development.[3]

This historical fact is one of the reasons why over-all community planning in intergroup relations has been retarded.

Aronson also points out that the development of private intergroup relations agencies for various so-called "minority" groups followed a similar but independent pattern. They progressed from the group welfare stage through the "defense" stage (during which they were "answering the bigot"); the "education" phase (during which they attempted to create a positive image in the public mind); the "intergroup cooperation" stage (during which councils were formed); the "social action" phase (when they were seeking governmental reform); and, finally, to "community relations" (in which the group seeks the maximum realization of its capacity to contribute toward the general welfare of society). He rightly points out that these phases are not separate and distinct, were not reached at the same time by each group, and that some of the agencies are continuing to carry on several of these phases at the same time.

Many of the private intergroup relations agencies that came into being between 1915 and 1940 resulted from

[3] Arnold Aronson, "Organization of the Community Relations Field," *ibid.*, p. 18.

specific events or situations, some terrifying, which brought forth the realization that there was a relationship between group welfare and community acceptance of individual rights and group differences. The *1959 Directory of Intergroup Relations Agencies* included an appendix, written by Frances R. Cousens and John G. Feild, which lists some of these events:

The 1921–24 Quota Laws saw the establishment of the Common Council for American Unity in 1921 and the International Institute movement in 1924. In addition, the American Jewish Congress, established first in 1917 as a temporary entity to affect the minority rights provisions of the Versailles Treaty, was reestablished on a permanent basis in 1922. The Scopes, Sweatt and other civil liberties trials saw the American Civil Liberties Union created in 1920. The American Association of Indian Affairs came into being two years before Indians were granted their citizenship in 1924. Changes in immigration laws regarding Orientals were connected with the origin of the Japanese American Citizens League in 1930. The Al Smith campaign led to the establishment of the National Conference of Christians and Jews in 1928. Concern with denial of voting rights, led U.S. Attorney General Frank Murphy to establish the Civil Rights Section in the Office of the Attorney General in 1939. The Fellowship House movement, the Catholic Interracial Council plan and the structure of the growing Jewish Community Relations Councils were all fairly well established by the end of the 1930's.[4]

Largely through the efforts of the private agencies concerned with group welfare and stimulated by President Roosevelt's Executive Order #8802 in 1941, we saw the emergence in the 1940s of local, state, and Federal governmental agencies. This set the stage for the explosive growth

[4] Frances R. Cousens and John G. Feild, "Some Observations on the Nature and Scope of Intergroup Relations," in *1959 Directory of Intergroup Relations Agencies* (New York: National Association of Intergroup Relations Officials, 1959), p. 78.

of those agencies that had a primary interest in civil rights and community relations. Some ninety governmental agencies have come into existence since 1943. Almost all of these public agencies were established as a result of social action efforts, stimulated by private agencies but joined by many civic, religious, labor, and community groups. In the main, they are administrative agencies, created by antidiscrimination legislation or ordinance, and have as their purpose the prevention or elimination of discrimination based upon race, religion, and national origin. They are obviously not group-oriented, as are the majority of private agencies, and they promote the public policy of equality of opportunity for all citizens.

These public agencies are legally constituted and, in most cases, administer laws which state the public policy to be one of nondiscrimination in specific areas of community life. Discrimination is an act against an individual because of his group identification. It is estimated that one half of the population of the United States now lives in states or municipalities covered by some form of antidiscrimination legislation, and each of these states or cities has an administrative intergroup relations agency. In addition to an enforcement responsibility, each of these governmental agencies is charged with the task of improving the relationships between groups and carrying on a broad educational program.

Public intergroup relations agencies are known by a variety of names, but most common is that of "Commission on Human Relations." A Commission on Human Relations is actually a citizen board appointed by the mayor or governor as the case may be. The members are selected as a cross section representation of the population in so far as the major religious, racial, and ethnic groups are concerned. They are status individuals. They meet regularly to review program, establish policy, and determine goals. In this capacity they act in the same manner and perform the same functions as the board of directors of any agency.

The Pittsburgh Commission, to choose an example, has fifteen members. In addition to meeting as a full Commission once a month, three standing committees each have one meeting a month. The Executive Committee is made up of the five elected officers and is responsible for recommending matters of policy to the Commission, coordinating the various phases of the total program, and, through the Executive Director, directing staff. A Case Conference Board of five members handles all the compliance activities, including complaints from individuals and groups. A Community Relations Board of five members reviews the community relations program of the Commission, including the neighborhood work, tension situations, cooperation with other agencies, and educational activities. Each of these committees is staffed by a professional worker. Commissioners, therefore, work on the operational as well as the policy level.

The chief functions of public intergroup relations commissions are:

1. *Enforcement.*—The one function which the public agency does not share with private intergroup agencies is that of securing compliance with laws against discrimination. However, the process used should be familiar to the social work field. The methods and techniques include: (1) investigation and fact finding; (2) negotiation; (3) persuasion; (4) conciliation; (5) private and public hearings;

and (6) possible legal action. The commission's action in such complaint cases is directed toward bringing about a change in practice in employment agencies, places of business and industry, trade and professional associations, institutions and labor unions. This largely involves working with policy-making officials. This phase of the work is not a police action but is designed to bring about change through understanding and acceptance of the public policy.

The public agency, however, cannot perform its compliance function without the help of other community groups and citizens. Thomas D. McBride, President of the Philadelphia Fellowship Commission, said at the 1961 annual meeting of that private agency:

> As we enter the 60's, it becomes clear that laws and public agencies can go just so far without intensive cooperation by citizens, organizations and the general public. The 60's, therefore, will depend more than ever upon private agencies to utilize the laws and, more importantly, motivate citizens to seek education and training requisite to take advantage of opportunities.[5]

2. *Research.*—Most public agencies do a certain amount of research. All of them study and investigate conditions that have an adverse effect on intergroup relations. The gathering and distribution of statistical data and case histories are not only of service to the public agency but to the private agencies and the community generally. There is need for frequent consultation with other agencies and community groups. Community welfare planning must start with such factual data and it must be shared. The Pittsburgh Commission has found that its studies on housing,

[5] Thomas D. McBride, "The Pendulum Swings," *Report to the Community,* XII (1961), 3.

education, hospital services, and the like have produced more tangible results in community planning and action than almost any other phase of its program.

3. *Education.*—This function requires interpretation of the public policy (equal opportunity for all) to as wide a public or to as various publics as is possible. It requires the use of mass media, the public rostrum, meetings with small and large groups, the preparation and use of visual materials and printed matter. To accomplish this function, a commission must seek and obtain the cooperation and resources of other community groups, individuals, and agencies.

The end sought is acceptance of the public policy and the development of a climate of opinion which makes it possible for those who favor it to comply with as little interference as possible. It seeks to decrease the number of persons who are unconcerned or who acquiesce without thinking in the traditional attitudes and practices which have made the enunciation of public policy necessary.

4. *Promotion of understanding.*—A function that comes close to social work objectives is that of promoting understanding among persons of different races, religions, and nationalities. This is accomplished through experience rather than through intellectual acceptance. Understanding is achieved by people working together on common problems or in conflict situations in which they have to make decisions concerning their own conduct and behavior, which may be modified by understanding through this experience. There is some of this in every situation involving a complaint case which is resolved by changing traditional patterns and bringing persons of different races or cultures together. It is present in conflict situations in neighbor-

hoods where there is a changing population, or where a non-white moves into a previously all-white area or block.

The reduction of intergroup conflict is brought about by making communication possible and by helping people of equal status to work together across lines of difference on matters of common interest or concern. As they learn to respect each other they not only begin to develop understanding but they also become concerned with one another's problems, including such things as discrimination and segregation.

Obviously, we have a social problem of considerable proportions. The problem concerns the worth and dignity of the individual and the growth of personality which is thwarted because of his identification with a so-called "minority" group. While social workers and social work agencies have traditionally fought social injustice, it is apparent from a review of the history of intergroup relations that they have not been particularly active in this field. Social workers have not identified the problem, have not pressed for social action, and have not mobilized community resources for the solution of the problem. The main drive for relief from this major social problem has come from religious, ethnic, and racial organizations. Public officials, being sensitive to the needs and demands of voters, and being responsible for maintaining law and order in their jurisdictions, have been receptive of civil rights legislation and the establishment of governmental administrative agencies.

In the present situation we find a great variety of groups operating outside the general community welfare structure to resolve this great problem of social injustice. In all the metropolitan areas and in many smaller communities as well we find public and private agencies and a growing number of community groups concerning themselves with one or more aspects of the intergroup relations program. Intergroup relations agencies, public and private, with full-time staff now have budgets which total approximately $25 million annually. This is a sizable operation to be ignored by the central social welfare planning bodies.

Mobility of population has long been characteristic of life in the United States. Most of the movement has been due to the natural desire of people to better themselves and to seek "greener pastures." This continues and includes now the movements of great numbers of people from depressed areas to areas of supposedly greater opportunity. Urbanization goes on apace; people from the central city are moving to suburbia; the central city is becoming the place of residence for the minority groups. Urban redevelopment and renewal, with the consequent population displacement and the disruption of social services and institutions, have intensified the problem. Minority groups, being the majority of displaced persons, are forced to move to other sections and to adjust to new neighbors—and the older residents of these areas to adjust to the newcomer.

Belatedly, social planners and physical planners are realizing that they must get together well before execution of redevelopment plans. Social planners bemoan the fact that they are not consulted before the drafting boards produce the physical plan that vitally affects the lives of people both in and out of the areas to be redeveloped. My contention is that both the physical and the social planner have failed to recognize the intergroup aspects of these population shifts. It is "later than you think" and well past the time when all the planners and representatives of the groups affected should together make a concerted effort at unified community welfare planning.

Gordon Manser says that as planning "councils place increasing emphasis upon community-wide problems, they logically perceive their constituency to be the entire community." [6] On the face of it, this would appear to be favorable to consideration of intergroup relations problems as a part of general community welfare planning. However, it would be favorable only if the planning council were truly representative of the whole community and if the council would recognize divergent and conflicting interests. This is not happening.

In my experience, the "association of givers" known in most communities as the United Fund has succeeded in involving in the policy positions persons highly placed in the community power structure. These persons are not social crusaders by any stretch of the imagination—they tend to maintain the status quo and they certainly avoid controversial issues. This is an extension to the higher community level of the same kind of conservatism that has faced social workers in their dealings with lay board members. They are in a position to determine to what purpose the "voluntary" funds are expended without the necessity of facing an electorate, as does the political officeholder, and they also control the purse strings of the welfare planning council. I am afraid that this precludes any serious consideration of including intergroup relations programs in the total community planning.

Mr. Manser is Executive Director of the Baltimore Council of Social Agencies. In a paper prepared for the United

[6] Gordon Manser, "A Critical Look at Community Planning," *Social Work,* V, No. 2 (1960), 36.

Community Funds and Councils of America in 1959, he analyzes the problems and the potential as well as the future of planning councils. In his entire paper he mentions not one word about any phase of intergroup relations problems. This is a discouraging lack of perception in our council leadership. The physical planners are learning that the whole program of urban redevelopment and renewal is about to founder on the rocks of restrictive housing practices in relation to the relocation of displaced families. Can it be that the social planners are behind even the physical planners in acceptance of the fact that intergroup relations problems are vitally affecting their work?

The coordination and planning for intergroup relations programs can be done by government, and at present that seems to be the trend. More and more, the private agencies and other groups are turning to the governmental administrative agency for this type of leadership. This is, however, a development that has come about through default and not because it is the desire of these agencies to separate themselves from the established community welfare councils. Neither is it the wise course of action, as witness the problems created for social planners by the independent decisions of the physical planners.

Events and conditions are rapidly approaching which will force community welfare councils to include intergroup relations concerns and programs in the total community planning. Just as redevelopment and renewal have produced concomitant social problems which welfare agencies have to handle, so the changes brought about by civil rights legislation and the pressure for equal treatment of minority groups in every area of community life bring the need for individual and group adjustments. Many of the institutions and agencies established to care for other welfare needs are facing radical adjustments in their service to clients, in their selection and training of staff, and even in board memberships. The question is whether planning councils will participate in planning for these social changes, or merely react to the changes as they occur.

I agree with a statement credited to the President of the Indianapolis Health and Welfare Council: "You cannot meet yesterday's problems today; you must meet *tomorrow's* problems *today*." As local community welfare councils come to grips with questions of broad social policy—and this includes intergroup relations policy—they are, in effect, accepting the validity of welfare planning as a proper community function.

PUBLIC AGENCY PARTICIPATION IN COMMUNITY PLANNING

by Richard S. Bachman

THE IMPORTANCE of participation by public, or tax-supported, agencies in local community planning is scarcely a debatable subject in modern social welfare. However, the quality or climate of such participation may be a wholly different matter.

First, let us dispose quickly of the logical necessity for such participation by public agencies. Social welfare represents, or should represent, an entity which places equal emphasis on all services without regard for their source of support. Modern social welfare planning starts with this concept. The importance of public agency participation in local planning is stressed by the American Public Welfare Association in its handbook for local public welfare directors. United Community Funds and Councils of America, Inc., in its pamphlet *Teamwork in Our Town* lists public agencies foremost under the heading, "Who Will Belong to the Council?"

Moving, then, to the climate or quality of public agency participation in local community planning, let us examine briefly some stages of development of typical local community welfare councils. (For this purpose I shall refer primarily to local planning as it is conducted by "community welfare councils," a term which includes welfare federations, united community councils, and related bodies.)

Even though community welfare councils antedated community chests or united funds in some cities, the councils traditionally have had a close relationship with the united funds and have received most of their financing from this source. The typical contract for participation in a fund calls for the agency to take part in local planning through the council. Thus, the private agencies which participate in united funds have constituted a large block of willing, or unwilling, members of councils.

Community welfare councils have been related closely to the budget problems of the united fund agencies either through actually doing the budgeting or serving in an advisory capacity. Budget committees of united funds have been a fertile source of referrals of problems as grist for the mill of the councils.

These relationships, coupled with major financial support of councils from united funds and frequent structural integration of funds and councils, have served to cloud the relationship between councils and public agencies. Public agencies, unlike united fund agencies, have no mandate, other than their own good judgment, to participate in local welfare planning. When they do take part in planning it is almost entirely on a staff level unless they can involve members of their advisory boards or commissions.

Some public agency executives seem to have a fixation about the laws and regulations which govern their programs. They are willing to meet with community groups to tell what their agencies can do or cannot do. Seldom are they genuinely willing to discuss modifications of their services to meet changing community needs, nor do they seem interested in enlisting support for necessary changes in the laws or regulations under which they operate. Fortunately, such people appear to be declining in numbers. We can hope that they will disappear.

A far larger group of public agency executives subscribe earnestly to the principle of participation in local planning. They are anxious to adjust their programs to existing or changing needs and to take part in research, planning, and forward-looking demonstration projects. They are limited in their own ability to engage in social action and to involve laymen or influential community groups but they recognize the potential ability of councils to engage in social action and to involve laymen or influential community groups.

Sometimes, members of this group of public administrators who participate in local community planning may feel frustrated or disappointed. Even though studies have demonstrated that tax money pays more than one half of the local health and welfare bill, they may think that community welfare councils are unduly preoccupied with the 5 percent of total costs paid by united funds. A few public agency executives have been known to state that they feel they are second-class citizens in their community welfare councils. It may seem to them that the councils are too wary about participation in legislative action because of fear that it may endanger the tax-exempt status of the council or that such activity may embarrass the united fund by offending substantial contributors. Or they may consider the council too naïve and inexperienced in political realities to be effective in the arena of practical and effective social action.

Are such situations inescapable or universal? In my experience and in my observations, they are not. Community welfare councils are "home-town products" in that they are completely autonomous. While they belong to United Community Funds and Councils of America, Inc., this national organization has no accrediting or chartering powers. Its powers are those of persuasion and education. However, most councils are staffed by trained people who have been developing through their national association and elsewhere a similar set of principles and objectives. So far as these staff people are concerned, there can be little doubt of their almost universal dedication to the principle of *at least* equal importance of their public and private member agencies. Some practical community considerations may cause them to seem to take an undue amount of time to study a relatively minor private agency. Yet this seemingly minor agency may lead to the involvement and education of influential community leaders on public and private problems. There is still the occasional council board member who wants to know what a legislative issue has to do with "our agencies," meaning the united fund agencies. Fortunately, such individuals are reaching the vanishing point among most council boards.

The Ohio Citizens' Council for Health and Welfare is very much interested in health and welfare legislation as part of its program. By policy, we work closely with the community welfare councils of at least twenty-three Ohio cities, covering about 80 percent of the population of our state.

From this vantage point we are able to observe the scope and nature of the interest of local councils in one state in the problems of their tax-supported agencies. A few brief examples will illustrate that these councils believe in public agency participation and that they work at it.

In Cleveland, much of the local financing of public assistance comes through special tax levies which have to be renewed periodically by the voters. In addition, Cleveland has had a series of bond issues for improvement or construction of public health and welfare facilities. For several years the Cleveland Welfare Federation has donated the full-time services of one of its associate directors for long periods as executive of the citizens' committees for these bond issues and levies. Their consistent success at the polls has been due in no small measure to this all-out support by the Welfare Federation.

In Dayton, the Community Welfare Council has had a contractual relationship with the urban renewal and redevelopment program to provide citizen interest and participation in this vital and often disruptive process. The principal contribution of the council has been through area councils to help the affected neighborhoods and agencies understand the process, prepare for it, and adjust to the inevitable changes.

In Columbus, the United Community Council has struggled actively and aggressively with a chronic problem of inadequate local financing for public assistance and periodic charges of "chiseling" by assistance recipients. The Council has spent endless hours of staff time with these problems and has enlisted active participation by top-level community leaders in the process. By no means have all the problems been solved, but unquestionably the situation would have been far worse without these activities. It is doubtful that the severest public agency critic of councils could have asked for any greater expenditure of time and effort by the Columbus Council.

In Akron, the United Community Council is embarking on an extensive and expensive study of local public welfare. Several Ohio councils study the local public agency budget proposals and appear at hearings in support of the budgets.

These few examples are taken from large cities, but the interest and activities are by no means confined to the metropolitan areas. In several of the smaller cities, the councils have provided the vehicles for help in financial crises, in mergers of city and county relief authorities, and in development of adequate detention facilities—to cite a few examples.

Most community welfare councils have been going through a transition in recent years. They tend to be less agency-centered and more problem-centered in their approach. In other words, they tend to think more in terms of major problems that involve large numbers of people and less in terms of relatively minor adjustments in agency programs. This leads inevitably to an increasing focus on public agencies since they involve the largest numbers of people and often have the greatest potential for growth through their broad base of tax support.

At the same time, councils have been increasingly successful in attracting the participation of major civic leaders who are essentially interested in broad, basic community problems.

Community welfare councils may be imperfect instruments in many instances, but they are the devices which have evolved on the American scene for local health and welfare planning. They are increasingly well staffed; gaining in community stature and influence; more problem-centered in their approach; and tend to rely more heavily on research and longer-range planning. Like all human institutions, they have a history which influences them to some degree. Usually they are expected to perform miracles with small budgets and no powers other than those of persuasion and the results of public opinion.

Sound social welfare planning can flourish only in a climate where all partners have equal status; where the impossible is not expected; where there is an atmosphere of mutual confidence and frank sharing of information or opinions; and where there is a willingness to modify programs and opinions on the basis of facts and sound planning. If councils and public agencies enter their relationships in this spirit, the gains will be to the communities and people they serve.

GOVERNMENTAL AND VOLUNTARY AGENCIES[1]

I. THEIR RESPECTIVE ROLES

by Alvin L. Schorr

IN DISCUSSING emerging patterns of relationship between governmental and voluntary agencies, we are dealing with a situation not unlike marriage. How does one achieve mutuality without discouraging difference? In reverse, how does a husband or wife achieve the fullest individuality without ignoring or overriding the spouse?

It seems to me that there are three issues currently involved in determining a pattern of mutuality; two of them are serious and one, at least in part, only semantic. First, one of the partners in this marriage of government and voluntarism is large, wealthy, and powerful. Government may have difficulties and strains of its own, but when there is an initial legislative decision, it tends to preempt the function involved, however large, and funds come forth. Though there are differences from state to state and from county to county, there is as much commonality as the government wishes to prescribe. The voluntary partner, on the other hand, is compact, various, and sensitive. There are a

[1] The views expressed are those of the author and do not necessarily represent the position of the Social Security Administration or of the Department of Health, Education, and Welfare.

variety of sponsorships for voluntary agencies—sectarian and secular, community-wide and more or less privately held, and local and national. Moreover, local units of a national organization will vary widely one from another. Though this is true of public agencies also, voluntary agencies are likely to consider variation and local sensitivity as a central part of their rationale and responsibility.

Some of the patterns that have emerged include collaborative relationships around services to a common client or regarding a common problem, contractual arrangements for the performance of services by voluntary agencies, mutual stimulation to improved service, and so on. This developing pattern may be evaluated by a criterion suggested by the differences of voluntary and public agencies, the criterion that a pattern ought to make the best use of each partner's unique situation. Viewed from the public agency's point of view, the pattern ought to provide true coverage for services that have come to be regarded as necessary. Moreover, it ought to do this without, in effect, absorbing or directing the major policies of the voluntary agencies. From the voluntary agency's point of view, the pattern ought to provide flexibility and sensitivity without requiring the voluntary agency to act as if the public agency is not there.

The second issue is really implicit in the differences that have been noted, and its nature can be appropriately stated in dollars and cents. In 1945 voluntary donors gave an estimated $790 million for a variety of welfare services, including family and child-care services, recreation, institutional care of the aged, maternity home care, and so forth.[2] In 1958, the year's contributions totaled about $1⅓ billion,[3]

[2] Thomas Karter, "Voluntary Agency Expenditures for Health and Welfare from Philanthropic Contributions, 1930–55," *Social Security Bulletin,* XXII, No. 2 (1958), 14–18.

[3] Estimate furnished by Thomas Karter, Division of Program Re-

an increase of 70 percent in a period during which the population had increased about 25 percent and prices 60 percent. In other words, voluntary contributions provided less real money per capita for welfare services in 1958 than in 1945 despite the fact that our skills had improved and the need for these tools seemed to have multiplied. (Within the general classification of welfare services, the lag in support is particularly striking for the casework services.) In consequence, voluntary agencies have been severely limited in what they might do, and they have been casting an increasingly speculative eye at the possible uses of public funds.

Money, as we know very well, exerts a powerful suction on services. (It is intended that it should; part of the purpose of grant programs and contracts is to interest voluntary agencies and independent professionals in doing work that the public finds important.) Here again, our criterion—that is, does a developing pattern make the best use of each partner's unique situation?—is applicable. Specifically, the public agency should ask itself whether it seeks relative uniformity and coverage in the use of its funds, or rather variety and concentrated attention in certain spots. If it seeks the former, it should do the job itself; if the latter, it might contract for service. Voluntary agencies are various in quality, as well as in other ways. The public agency must ask itself also what standards it expects and how they will be assured. The voluntary agency, for its part, must ask whether it fulfills a special role in contracting to provide a service or is simply being seduced by the availability of money, whether carelessly or at its own ardent entreaty. Such narrower questions as these may be used as a test:

search, Office of the Commissioner, Social Security Administration, Department of Health, Education, and Welfare.

What is special about our function now *because* we are voluntary? If we take on this job, how will this affect or displace other aspects of our program? To what degree are we in accord with the conditions as to standards and reporting which we shall be required to meet? Shall we be free, after a year or a decade, to shift our program, if this seems desirable, or will it turn out that we have no other sources of support?

The third issue is one that I consider to be semantic and, in part, unreal. When public agencies did little or nothing, there was no problem of distinguishing them from voluntary agencies. When they did much, though poorly, the distinction was stated in these terms, somewhat dressed up for decency: the public agencies did the coverage job and the voluntary agencies the experimentation and trail blazing. Now, public agencies also on occasion experiment and blaze trails, and we are left with the feeling that things are not neat. There is duplication, and that must mean that there is waste. But perhaps duplication serves a purpose.

We are all troubled, voluntary and public agencies alike, by the degree to which our work becomes formalized. We are borne down with forms and statistics, and constricted in proper channels of communication. There are few places where we can say that our organization and techniques are designed precisely to deal with our current clientele. I do not mention this to imply that we wish it so; these developments are perhaps inevitable companions of size, pressure, and professionalization. But it seems dangerous to seek too much tidiness in the face of these developments. There is merit in side-by-side performance of the same jobs, if there may be competition and if variation, whether planned or accidental, stimulates examination of the way we work.

Here, of course, I am reviving the "yardstick" concept of public-voluntary relationship; the only novelty is that I think it ought to measure both ways—the voluntary should measure up to the public as well as vice versa.

So much for mutuality; but not *all* is mutuality. If we stipulate that there must be partnership and respect, we also recognize that public and voluntary agencies are independent of and may view each other critically. In the earnest work to which we are dedicated, respect is hardly possible without criticism. It seems to me that this is a central function of voluntary agencies. The nature of the growth of public welfare, so frequently by means of specific measures taken in answer to specific critical needs, leads to programs that have gaps and may be uncoordinated. Eventually, there comes a call for coordination and rationalization, but any large change requires a new adjustment among the various agencies, groups of clients, and political forces that may be involved. Thus criticism is required—criticism that is fundamental, convincing, and vigorous.

Such criticism may, as they say about conversation, be an expiring art among us. At any rate, it seems to me that it is only rarely forthcoming from voluntary agencies about public agencies. It is as if we had agreed that there should be criticism on just certain matters. For example, we are willing to have categories in public assistance criticized; criticism of residence requirements is also acceptable. But there are other matters about which voices are rarely raised. For example, something between a fourth and a fifth of the nation's children—let us say 14 million children—are in low-income families.[4] This is many more children by far

[4] Robert J. Lampman, "The Low Income Population and Economic Growth," prepared for the Joint Economic Committee, Study Paper No. 12, Joint Committee Print, 86th Congress, 1st session; and Lenore

than would receive public assistance under any of the proposals for liberalization that have so far been put forward. Moreover, a public assistance program that reached 14 million children would have a different philosophy from our present program which, large though it is, is regarded as residual. There has not been debate about these children or about what type of program may reach them, though voluntary agencies deal with these children and their families every day. It is perhaps to be expected that public agencies should fail to worry about the 14 million children; they are heavily burdened in trying to help roughly one fourth of that number. Moreover, questions are useful only if they lead to proposals, and public agencies are limited in what they may propose. But what limits the vigor with which voluntary agencies may address themselves to the need of these children?

Perhaps this is an unfair example. It has been argued that social and economic reform in the United States, as in the rest of the Western world, is now largely a by-product of economic progress. There is a tacit political truce, writes Gunnar Myrdal,[5] and no longer a real struggle to achieve a more just distribution of national income. (It is an interesting confirmation of this point that, though we have heard at this Conference a good deal of firm resolve to wipe out poverty, we have heard no proposals for redistribution. The difference between redistributing wealth and waiting for increased wealth to filter down to poor people is, of course, a substantial difference in tempo.) If this is so, then reliance on large-scale economic progress eventually to resolve the problem of so many children is not peculiar to

A. Epstein, "Some Effects of Low Income on Children and Their Families," *Social Security Bulletin*, XXIV, No. 2 (1961), 12–17.

[5] Gunnar Myrdal, *Beyond the Welfare State* (New Haven, Conn.: Yale University Press, 1960).

social welfare. Let me offer another example, in the area of practice rather than of broad programing.

As public welfare's concerns are legally prescribed, and frequently acute besides, public agency workers are likely to have a considerable sense of urgency about the problems with which they deal. At the same time, other problems may seem to them to be relatively unimportant. This is at the heart of the complaint that voluntary agencies exercise finer and finer skills upon the increasingly esoteric problems of fewer and fewer people. Voluntary agency people, for their part, have the opportunity to view the programs of public agencies with somewhat similar detachment and to feel urgency about other kinds of problems.

It seems to me that the urgency that many public agencies feel about the problems they face is increasingly being reinforced by the desperation of voluntary agencies about the same problems. I have in recent months seen material on multiple-problem families that defines them as virtually identical with public assistance families. Where are the single-problem families of yesteryear? Or were there never any? Having thus circularly defined public assistance families as multiple-problem, and by simple elision hard-to-reach, we set out to compel change from them. I do not dismiss this problem lightly or say that there is not reason for our concern, but there is danger in this kind of categorization as well. I have argued, for example, that it is among the factors that are leading social work to an increasingly prescriptive, coercive practice.[5] It is natural that public welfare agencies should be acutely concerned about the very real problems with which they deal. Should we not

[5] Alvin L. Schorr, "Trend to Rx," paper presented at the George Warren Brown Alumni Seminar, Minneapolis, June, 1960; scheduled for publication in *Social Work*.

expect, however, that the voluntary agencies will find time to pause, will call not for more wholesale and more powerful methods, but for care, for discrimination, for individualization?

I will not labor this point. I am merely trying to say that I regard it as a responsibility of voluntary agencies to criticize what public programs do and how they do it. I speak of serious criticism, not petty and neither friendly nor unfriendly, but based firmly on the consciousness that it is the needy or the troubled whom we all serve, not a voluntary organization or a public one. Such criticism as we have had has in recent years been bland and repetitious. I suspect that this is not for lack of more to question.

I set out to discuss mutuality and independence in the relations of public and voluntary agencies, and probably I have not made a clean distinction. To achieve mutuality presupposes that the partners understand their independent roles. At any rate, we have a dynamic interaction of independent partners. If we proceed with respect, with understanding, and with primary dedication to our mission to heal and to prevent, this partnership will provide a force for work that is complete and that continually improves itself.

II. A STUDY OF LAY AND PROFESSIONAL ATTITUDES

by Ralph M. Kramer

AMONG THE MORE SIGNIFICANT developments taking place in the field of social welfare is the changing relationship between public and voluntary agencies, manifested particularly in the blurring of differences between them. There seems to be substantial agreement in the professional literature that, as a result of a continual merging of function and interest, it is now much less possible to find distinguishing differences between public and voluntary agencies in terms of role, skills, goals, or "pioneering." Support for this point of view can be found in the recent writings of Arlien Johnson, Leonard Mayo, Donald S. Howard, Samuel Mencher, George Davidson, and Lester Granger.[1]

At the same time, however, considerable concern has been expressed about the future of health, welfare, and recreation services under voluntary auspices. The proposed study of the Rockefeller Foundation under the direction of Dr. Robert Hamlin is one reflection of this.

Three sets of factors are frequently cited as indication of a need for reevaluation of the respective roles of public and voluntary agencies: (1) the growing complexity, specialization, and professionalization of social welfare; (2) the diminution of functional differences between them—public agencies, for example, continually take over services that were formerly under voluntary auspices; (3) such fiscal trends as:

[1] Arlien Johnson, "Public Funds for Voluntary Agencies," *The Social Welfare Forum, 1959* (New York: Columbia University Press, 1959), pp. 83–102; Leonard Mayo, "The Changing Role of Voluntary Agencies," *Social Work Journal,* (1955), 95–103; Donald S. Howard, "Changing Roles of Public and Private Social Welfare Agencies," *The Social Welfare Forum, 1952* (New York: Columbia University Press, 1952), pp. 232–50; Samuel Mencher, "The Future for Voluntaryism in American Social Welfare," in Alfred S. Kahn, ed., *Issues in American Social Work* (New York: Columbia University Press, 1959), pp. 219–41; George F. Davidson, "Responsibility to Meet Social Service Needs," in James E. Russell, ed., *National Policies for Education, Health and Social Services* (New York: Doubleday and Company, 1955), pp. 151–72; Lester B. Granger, "The Changing Functions of Voluntary Agencies," in Cora Kasius, ed., *New Directions in Social Work* (New York: Harper, 1954), pp. 68–86.

(*a*) an expenditure-growth rate of public agencies which is almost three times that of voluntary agencies; (*b*) increasing availability of tax funds to voluntary agencies; (*c*) incapacity of voluntary agencies to increase real income much beyond the present level.

These changes not only challenge some of the traditional attitudes and concepts regarding public and voluntary agencies, but also raise many policy and social planning questions: Is a division of responsibility between public and voluntary agencies possible? Should the relationship between them be supplementary or complementary in character? Is there a need for a new rationale for the voluntary agency in the future? What are some of the implications for voluntarism?

The answers to these and related questions have many implications for the future course and character of social welfare in the United States, in addition to their consequences for budgeting and planning. An analysis of public-voluntary relationships may also contribute toward the formulation of a general theory of social welfare.

Before one might suggest what the relationship between public and voluntary agencies *can* be, however, one requires objective information as to what it actually *is*. Unfortunately, there is a paucity of the empirical studies that are necessary to provide a better understanding of these issues. It would be very helpful, if not essential, for instance, to know something about the beliefs of agency leadership—how do the leaders view the roles of, and relationship between, public and voluntary agencies? The assumption here is that the values and attitudes of the public and voluntary leadership are of considerable importance in decision-making and, therefore, in agency policy formulation.

I shall describe some of the results of an exploratory study aimed at learning, for the first time, the opinions of a representative sample of 150 professional and lay leaders (executives and presidents) of public and voluntary agencies in the San Francisco Bay Area. Through interviews, seven interrelated aspects of public-voluntary relationships were covered. These were: (1) distinguishing characteristics of public and voluntary agencies (strengths and weaknesses of each); (2) appropriate roles and relationships; (3) the effect of public or voluntary auspices; (4) the use of tax funds by voluntary agencies; (5) a division of responsibility between public and voluntary agencies; (6) a concept of social welfare; and (7) the ideology of humanistic liberalism.

These seven issues were developed from a review of 240 items found in the professional literature on this subject during the last forty years and provide a way to classify those recurring themes in the literature, in other words, the most frequently discussed aspects of the topic and those which appear to be central to an understanding of this subject.

While the content of the opinions of agency leadership on characteristics, interrelationships, and the structure of their beliefs was of major interest, it was also possible to test a series of hypotheses pertaining to specific differences in the ways in which professionals and volunteers would perceive these issues.

Based on a review of the literature, a list of close to two hundred questions was prepared which covered the seven major issues. The list was then submitted to a group of experts in the San Francisco Bay Area for a judgment as to adequacy of scope and content. In the course of twenty-two trial interviews, the schedule was revised six times and in its final form, contained twenty-four open-end questions which required about an hour-long interview and verbatim recording.

In selecting the sample, "public agencies" were defined as the following: health, welfare, probation, park, and recreation departments in the five Bay Area counties of San Francisco, Alameda, Contra Costa, Marin, and San Mateo; and, in addition, the Area offices of three state departments (Health, Social Welfare, and Recreation) and five Federal agencies under the Department of Health, Education, and Welfare. Thirty-four agency directors (professionals) and sixteen laymen were commission chairmen in this group, and all were included in the sample, making a total of fifty from the public agencies.

The universe from which the voluntary health, welfare, and recreation agencies was drawn was defined as those receiving funds from the United Bay Area Crusade. This was in addition to the presidents and executive directors of the five county fund-raising, budgeting, and planning bodies, all of whom were included, making a total of thirty-one in this particular group. Several of the large, independent health agencies which were not receiving United Crusade funds were also included in order to fill out the health sample.

The method chosen to select the voluntary agency presidents and executives was that of disproportional stratified sampling with the final choice being a random selection.

Through a contract with a market and survey research firm, seven women interviewers were selected, only two of whom had any previous experience in the field of social welfare. They were ostensibly chosen for their demonstrated skill in depth interviewing and verbatim recording. A set of orientation and background materials was prepared for their study beforehand, and a four-hour training session was conducted prior to the actual interviewing.

All respondents received a letter describing the purposes of the survey and a copy of some of the questions before the interviewer phoned to request an appointment. There were only three refusals, and ten substitutions. All the interviews were completed during January, 1959.

For many of the respondents, the interview seemed to serve as an educational and clarifying experience. Many volunteered the information that the interview had improved their own understanding of the issues. Few seemed to have given the subject much thought prior to receipt of the questions, although virtually all expressed rather well-formulated opinions during the interview. Several executives and board presidents used the questions for discussion at board meetings.

The coding categories were developed from an *a posteriori* content analysis of the completed schedules. Coding and tabulation were completed by two senior staff members of the research organization.

Before summarizing some of the preliminary findings, it should be stressed that the tabulated data have not been completely analyzed and that the following report is based only on a comparison of the opinions of professionals and volunteers in public and voluntary agencies; there has not yet been a breakdown by fields of service, counties, or personal attributes.

Also, while some statistically significant findings at the 5 percent level of confidence emerged, generalizations as to other communities should probably be made with much more caution. The degree to which these expressed attitudes reflect Bay Area experience and the traditional service pattern in each county is not known. For this reason, replication of the survey in other metropolitan areas would be most desirable.

The following are some of the tentative findings to-date:

1. *Distinguishing characteristics of public and voluntary agencies.*—Volunteers tended to cite more people-centered qualities, such as the opportunity for citizen participation and the more personal nature of the agency's services, as the major advantages of the voluntary agency. Professionals described the distinctive strengths of the voluntary agency in such agency-centered terms as flexibility and the ability to experiment. Very few saw the voluntary agency as a bulwark against further encroachment of government, as a standard-setter, or as an instrument which provided an opportunity for choice of service. Almost all the professionals and volunteers could cite specific examples of the pioneering role of the voluntary agency, although the term was very loosely construed. Most preferred to use the term "voluntary" rather than "private," although proportionally more professionals preferred the latter.

The outstanding disadvantage of the voluntary agency as perceived by both professionals and volunteers was its inadequate and unstable financal base. The special difficulties of working with volunteers were a secondary disadvantage in the eyes of the volunteers, while the professionals were also critical of the inadequate and inefficient services of voluntary agencies.

Both volunteers and professionals described the strengths of the public agency in similar terms: its secure financial base in tax support; broad scope of service; and legal responsibility. Disproportionately more professionals were aware that public agencies experiment with or demonstrate new services; very few volunteers had ever heard about this function. The most frequently mentioned disadvantages of the public agency cited by the volunteers were those attributed to its bureaucratic nature: wastefulness; inefficiency; bigness and impersonalness; as well as political manipulation. Curiously, lack of citizen participation was the item least mentioned by the volunteers. It was not surprising that the majority of the volunteers, in contrast to the professionals, thought that many public welfare programs encouraged dependency and that public assistance was a privilege and not a right. Professionals, however, tended to ascribe the inherent weaknesses of the public agency to poor quality of staff, inflexible administration, and obsolete laws and regulations.

The blurring of traditional lines between public and voluntary agencies was evident in the frequency with which each was defined in terms of one to the other. Both groups showed a rather surprising willingness to generalize about the characteristics of public and voluntary agencies, and expressed little recognition of the many differences within each group. Also noteworthy was the great emphasis given by leadership to the crucial significance of financial factors.

2. *Appropriate role and relationships.*—Professionals and volunteers tended to see the demonstration or "vanguard" function of voluntary agencies as of great importance, but a majority of the volunteers, particularly those in the public agencies, were hesitant to endorse this function if it meant that the demonstrated service would be taken over by a public agency. Professionals in the voluntary agencies approved while those in public agencies disapproved of this role of the voluntary agency. While the "vanguard" con-

cept was asserted by many, there was no mention of such traditional role theories as the "parallel bars," "extension ladder," and so on.

There was general agreement that both public and voluntary agencies are necessary because of their unique characteristics—"each can do certain things best"—as well as because of the existence of a vast range of unmet social needs. Both saw the relationship between public and voluntary agencies as supplementary, as a partnership. In comparing the two kinds of agencies, the majority of the respondents would not generalize as to which was "more effective" or "better understood or accepted," although volunteers tended to favor the voluntary agency slightly on these items. Significantly more volunteers than professionals, however, tended to believe that the voluntary agencies have higher standards of service and personnel. The professionals, in general, avoided such blanket statements, and were not as "voluntary agency-centered" as the volunteers in making such comparative judgments.

The majority of the volunteers expressed a preference for *only* the voluntary agency to grow, while professionals were more interested in the expansion both of voluntary and of public agencies. Both agreed that there was an inexorable trend toward the growth of public agencies, probably at the expense of the voluntary agency. The volunteers seemed to manifest more faith in the future of the voluntary agency, but they saw less need to support this conviction that "it was not on the way out." Some of their optimism and confidence in the future of the voluntary agency was tempered by the lack of coordination among agencies and the perennial problems of federated financing. It was characteristic of both groups to reject the purported solution of government financing of most voluntary agencies, although the volunteers expressed more emotional and ideological objections. While aware of these differences in capacity to deal effectively with present problems, both groups tended to regard working relationships between public and voluntary agencies as satisfactory and not in need of any special attention.

Thus, with regard to these interrelated issues—characteristics, role, and relationships—the professional and volunteer leadership viewed the relationship between public and voluntary agencies as a partnership, one supplementing the other. The differences between professionals and volunteers were not as pronounced on these issues as they were on the others: they both tended to perceive the characteristics, role, and relationships as affecting public and voluntary agencies in similar terms, but attached slightly differing degrees of importance and emphasis. The volunteers described these aspects in more personal, general, and somewhat ideological terms; in contrast to the professionals, who were a little more cautious about generalizing, not as voluntary agency-centered, although more agency- than people-centered.

3. *The effect of public or voluntary auspices.*—The volunteers tended to believe that auspices do make a considerable difference to people and that the voluntary agency is preferred. The professionals viewed auspice as just another variable, comparable to, but no more significant than, agency size, quality of staff, or administration.

Significantly more professionals than volunteers recommended the transfer of over fifty specific services currently under voluntary auspices to public agency auspices on the grounds that they might be more effectively administered. Only public agency leadership recommended the transfer of auspices from public to voluntary, but there was consensus among all against a shift of social agency services to more primary social institutions, such as the church, neighbors, the family.

4. *The use of tax funds by voluntary agencies.*—Almost all professionals and volunteers favored the use of tax funds by voluntary agencies, particularly in the form of contracts and grants for construction, demonstration, and research. There were very few who maintained that public funds should only be administered by public agencies. Some were even in favor of subsidies, although this was opposed to the greatest extent by the public agency professionals.

5. *A division of responsibility between public and voluntary agencies.*—In contrast to the considerable interest in this issue on the part of social planning bodies, only a very small majority of professionals and volunteers saw any necessity in attempting to formulate a division of labor between public and voluntary agencies by fields of service. A large number believed that such a determination was neither necessary, desirable, nor practical, on the grounds that the status quo was satisfactory or that such an effort might lead to an even greater assumption of responsibility by government. There was agreement, however, that if this task were undertaken, social planning organizations should take the initiative.

6. *A concept of social welfare.*—Most volunteers expressed a marked preference for a "residual" conception of social welfare, while most of the professionals preferred the "institutional" concept.[2]

7. *The ideology of humanistic liberalism.*—Character-

[2] Harold L. Wilensky and Charles N. Lebaux, *Industrial Society and Social Welfare* (New York: Russell Sage Foundation, 1958), p. 138.

istically, more professionals than volunteers expressed humanistic views regarding the nature of man, and a liberal view of government and its responsibilities. The professionals tended to be less concerned about the growing role of government in American life, the expansion of public agencies, and the increasing professionalization of the social services. Volunteers were inclined to believe that help to troubled persons is too easily available, and they placed less emphasis on the values of self-determination than did the professionals.

What might explain the relatively small number of statistically significant differences between professionals and volunteers in their attitude toward public and voluntary agencies? The following possibilities may exist:

a) The professional and volunteer leadership do not differ substantially in their attitudes toward these issues; that is, the original hypothesis is *not* supported.

b) The questions were poorly phrased and did not tap the true differences which exist.

c) While leadership verbalizes relative agreement in principle, in actual practice, in policy formulation, they would express different attitudes.

d) They hold similar attitudes, but for different reasons.

Perhaps further analysis of the data and additional studies of decision-making might throw more light on this.

The fact that the respondents did not express the expected degree of difference of opinion may be related to the absence of a sense of crisis, of a need to change, or that degree of discomfort usually expressed as "something's wrong" or "something ought to be done." The voluntary agency leadership seems to identify only one major problem, and it is primarily a fiscal one whose solution simply requires additional funds and little soul searching or change. Thus, there seems to be a general lack of awareness of some of those trends which have been identified, at least in the literature, as endangering the future healthy growth of the voluntary agency. Is this complacency found in other metropolitan areas?

To summarize the tentative conclusions of the survey:

1. In the San Francisco Bay Area, status as a professional or volunteer is more significant as a determinant of attitude than the type of agency, public or voluntary, with which leadership is associated. That is, there were more differences *between* all professionals and volunteers than *within* the agencies' leadership.

2. There are marked ideological differences between professionals and volunteers, and the consequences and implications are not yet clear. These differences pertain to opposing conceptions of social welfare, of the role of government, and of human nature. With regard to certain aspects of humanistic liberalism, professionals and volunteers manifest two contrasting sets of attitudes. Those findings also corroborate the results of Nettler's child welfare opinion study in Houston.[3] Incidentally, among the four scales which he used—determinism, punitiveness, perception of need, and method of financing—Nettler found that the difference regarding tax versus voluntary financing was the most consistent and most crucial one among the lay leaders and professional staff. He further noted that the voluntary-minded do not see as much "need" as the tax-minded.

3. While there are these valuative differences between

[3] Gwynn Nettler, "A Study of Opinions on Child Welfare in Harris County" (Houston, Texas: Community Council of Houston and Harris County, 1958), p. 98.

professionals and volunteers, both tend to view public and voluntary agency relationships in somewhat the same general ways.

4. Both professionals and volunteers tend to perceive social welfare in holistic rather than dualistic terms. The welfare dollar is conceived as a unity, and there is little aversion to the use of tax dollars by voluntary agencies—indeed, there is quite a readiness for it.

5. There seems to be little recognition that voluntarism or the voluntary agency may be threatened or that a new rationale may be needed for the voluntary agency today. Both the professional and the volunteer leadership appear to be quite complacent about the future of the voluntary agency and rather unconcerned about the relationship between public and voluntary agencies. They do not see this relationship as particularly crucial or in need of review or change. Instead, both groups tend to accept the status quo and see only a healthy and appropriate partnership in which the voluntary agency supplements the public agency.

There is a great emphasis by both on the central importance of inadequate funds: "If only more money were available . . ." There appears to be little recognition of the necessity for reevaluation of function, planning, research, or the determination of its division of responsibility.

All of these could well constitute hypotheses which could be used as a basis for further studies. Among some of the other research avenues which might be pursued are the following:

1. A similar attitude survey could be conducted among agency leadership in other communities in different parts of the country to see if these results are duplicated. This may also give us further understanding of the extent to

which one's attitudes are related to one's status as a professional or volunteer, and the extent to which they are influenced by local community factors. Other studies might focus their questions around a service-centered approach rather than the agency-centered one described here. Also, it might be interesting to see the results if the sample were chosen on a random basis and if multiple-choice questions were used.

2. Several case studies might be made of the dynamics of public-voluntary agency interaction in a community, such as a public welfare department and a family service agency; a public recreation department and a YMCA; a county hospital and sectarian hospital.

3. The relationship between the role of ideology of leadership and specific policy decisions affecting public-voluntary agency relationships could be studied in a situational context to answer the question: To what extent *does* ideology influence decisions?

4. In addition to these empirical studies, the literature should be reviewed, and an historical study similar to the English work of Madeline Rooff,[4] might be rewarding.

5. Finally, an analysis of the criteria for a division of responsibility between public and voluntary agencies which have been developed by social planning bodies would be a most useful guide to future policy formation in this area.

[4] Madeline Rooff, *Voluntary Societies and Social Policy* (London: Routledge and Kegan Paul, 1957).

PROBLEMS AND DIRECTIONS IN HEALTH PLANNING

by Gaylord W. Anderson, M.D.

THE PRINCIPAL PROBLEMS of health planning arise from the necessity of dealing with people. The biggest single problem is that different people have different ideas, based on differences in social, economic, and political philosophy. Although we all say glibly that we seek health for all persons and even subscribe to the World Health Organization goal of social, physical, and mental well-being, nonetheless our definition of the parameters of this goal may not be identical, and this lack of agreement will of necessity be reflected in our planning. It should not be inferred that I believe these differences to be undesirable or that I necessarily look upon them as a hindrance; for they more likely serve as a much needed brake upon hasty and precipitous action that we might regret in the light of subsequent events or even sober reflections.

"Direction" is more difficult of definition, but it is closely related to the problems. If it were possible for us to sit down in the awesome silence of isolation from world affairs, planning would be simple. We might map out a series of steps toward utopia and limit our discussion to the several paths that we might follow in this mythical journey. Bold reality tells us, however, that our health planning can never be so simple or idealistic but rather will be governed by the social, biological, and technological forces that are operating within our society. These forces are constantly creating new problems faster than we can solve the old. The direction of our health planning is thus governed not by what you and I as amateur social philosophers would like to envision but rather by the unending flow of events and the pressures of various forces that bring us face to face with problems that we might wish to avoid. It is a trite but nonetheless true statement that we are dealing with evolutionary forces and that our problems and the direction of our health planning are governed more by those forces than by any alternatives that the human mind can conceive.

If we may then concede that the problems of health planning that confront us in the social welfare field are the inevitable consequence of fundamental evolutionary forces beyond our control, let us look briefly at a few of these for the solution of which planning is essential in the years that are ahead.

The past century has witnessed an almost alarming rate of progress in the physical sciences, a rate that has rapidly accelerated in each succeeding decade. In a single decade of the present century man has made more scientific progress than in the entire span of time prior to the nineteenth and possibly even the twentieth century. As an inevitable sequel to these discoveries and their application to human affairs, there have been profound changes in our social and economic structure, as well as the creation of new health problems directly related to these discoveries.

The fundamental changes in transportation have created many new health problems. Infectious diseases that were at one time confined to specific geographical areas, and which moved slowly or not at all from one area to another, have today become international travelers and at any time may appear where heretofore they have been unknown. The past quarter century has witnessed several episodes of this character; at least two of these, had the challenge not been met by prompt recognition of the problem and effective planning, might have created disasters such as have not been known since the plagues of the Middle Ages.

We do not need to travel to distant lands to witness the impact of transportation upon our health problems. In our own backyards we have witnessed the growth of suburbia. Much has been written about the social and educational problems arising from this mushroom growth and about the economic plight of the cities from which the suburbanites have moved. Far less has been said of the present and future health problems that face those areas where, with flimsy, jerry-built housing and no proper concern for sanitation, we are creating tomorrow's slums that we shall bequeath to our children as an unwelcome inheritance and a testimonial to our lack of foresight or of concern for the future. Unfortunately, the forces that have brought about this mushrooming suburbia are beyond the control of health or social planning. Consequently, serious problems have been wished upon us without our being empowered to take the steps that are necessary to prevent them. I need only refer to the shocking negligence of suburban communities with respect to such basic necessities as safe water and proper sewage disposal. The problems of unplanned suburbia are upon us today and are likely to afflict the nation well beyond our lifetime.

One more example from the technological field will suffice—the potential health problems consequent upon the discoveries of nuclear physics. I am not a prophet of disaster, nor am I concerned with the awesome threat that some would attribute to the mere testing of atomic weapons. Quite apart from these problems in which moral philosophy becomes inseparably intertwined with scientific reasoning, the fact remains that the coming decades are bound to be marked by tremendous advances in the peaceful uses of atomic energy. The physical forces here do indeed present hazards. Fortunately in this field, in which the avarice of real estate operators and contractors and the stupidity of village officials and residents have not entered as in suburbia, intelligent planning has been possible and has prevailed with the result that, concomitant with the increase in nuclear hazards, we are going to witness the development of effective control programs. I am confident that when, in due course, our children look back upon the next few decades they will note striking examples of intelligent planning brought about by the recognition of problems as well as of tendencies that contribute to the growth of problems.

Just as we have been aware of trends in physical sciences that have created health problems, so also have we seen the effect of biological forces. Much has been written upon communicable disease control and its effect on the age distribution of our population. Countless millions of persons, who would have died as children or as young adults, had the impact of infection not been controlled, have been spared. As a consequence, we have seen a shift of population into the older age groups where the degenerative diseases constitute problems that lend themselves more to control than to prevention. At the same time, however, we have witnessed an even more significant shift of population into the younger ages. If, through control of infections such as infant diarrhea, malaria, childhood tuberculosis, and the like, children are spared to grow up to the age of reproduction, two consequences will inevitably follow.

The first of these is that the number of births will rise so that a greater proportion of our total population will be found in the years of childhood. Thus, apart from social and economic factors that are reflected in the birth rate, there is the simple fact that more people will be in the age of reproduction than there were in the era when childhood deaths were so common. The inevitable result will be an increase rather than a decrease in the magnitude of child health problems.

We have been so pleased with our accomplishments in the control of infectious diseases and the reduction of infant mortality that we have too often been lulled into overlooking the serious effects on child health and development. Here again the direction of our planning is influenced not by our ideas as to desiderata but rather by the realization that there will be a striking increase in the number of children for whom care must be provided. When we realize that these children, the product of birth rates of around 25 per 1000 population, will within two decades be the reproductive segment of the population (as contrasted to the current reproductive segment produced by birth rates around 18 per 1000), we are forced to look forward to even greater problems of child health and protection in a very few years when the child group will be from 30 percent to 50 percent larger than at present.

Inextricably interlocked with this problem is the unpleasant question of population control. It has been customary to portray public health as the glamorous knight errant, clad in gleaming armor (either aseptic or antiseptic) and carrying the spear of modern science, riding forth to slay the vile dragon of disease. To public health, therefore, has been accorded an aura of glory and triumph for its accomplishments. None of us would for the moment begrudge recognition for past or current accomplishments, for we cherish human life and accept a moral obligation to share our scientific knowledge and skill with all peoples. Yet the fact remains that those very triumphs of preventive medicine and public health are of necessity bringing about a so-called "population explosion" that will cause major health problems for future generations. In past times the Four Horsemen of destruction have ridden through the world, keeping down the population through famine, war, and disease. The conquest of diseases which killed in childhood can only mean that millions of children whom we would have lost in yesteryear will soon be the parents of tomorrow and their progeny, also spared the ravages of childhood deaths, will in their due time add to the overcrowding of population. We rejoice at the conquest of malaria, which one time killed as many as 2,000,000 children a year in India alone, but we recognize the impact on an already overcrowded subcontinent that will be caused by the added child population of the future. Thus public health, formerly cast as a glorious hero in the human drama, now appears in a far less glamorous role, and in some respects may be regarded by certain persons as a subtle villain whose deeds may ultimately compound the difficulties that beset the human race.

I doubt if any of us would suggest that we should scrap our health programs, return to the days when infection was rampant, when half of the newborn babies died in the first year of life, when those who survived were too often the victims of crippling illness. We would not callously deny the mother of far-off lands the opportunity of saving her child even though she may have achieved a certain degree of stoicism toward its death.

Rather than adopt such an approach which offends our sense of moral values, we must find acceptable methods of population control, lest we bequeath to those who come after us a serious and even frightening problem of over-population, which will beget wars with all the horror that these imply in this nuclear age. I realize full well that any suggestion of population control of necessity touches upon very fundamental differences in religious beliefs. I respect these beliefs just as deeply as do those who hold them and would be the last to intimate that any step should be contemplated which would force upon a person or a people any course contrary to his religious beliefs or spiritual convictions. Yet, I recognize that throughout the world there are profound differences in social customs and religious tenets. While I do not accept these foreign doctrines for my own life, I have the most profound respect for those who cling to concepts that are so different from mine and respect their right to live by these tenets even though I do not agree with them.

Since moral concepts as applied to population control are not uniform throughout the world, or even within a given country, I can recognize that methods of population control that would be inacceptable to one social or religious philosophy would be acceptable and even desirable to another. There is no thought on my part that any one universally acceptable plan of population control should or even could be developed; for each culture, each religion, each civilization, must obviously live and act within its own moral and social tenets. The problem is not simple, but we would be highly remiss in our obligation to coming generations if we were to continue to ignore this threat of overpopulation which will face the world in a future which is uncomfortably near. It is not too early to plan so that every culture will find a solution compatible with its own tenets.

A third health problem created by this control of infant mortality and infectious disease is that of old age and the degenerative diseases. Much has been written, and far more will be written, regarding the serious situation created by the fact that so large a fraction of our population is surviving to the age of physical incapacity and even senility. I am not referring to our physically active and mentally alert senior citizens, but rather to the growing number of persons who have reached the age at which the deterioration of the human body has reduced them to varying degrees of dependence. And I am recognizing the fact that while the problem is already one of considerable magnitude, this same problem will be much greater when our children and our grandchildren will be wondering what to do with you and me in our senility.

Here we must plan for hospitalization, for home care, for medical and nursing services over and above mere housing, clothing, and feeding. Unfortunately, just as we know that plans for population control involve fundamental differences in religious and moral beliefs, so must we recognize that in planning for the care of the aged we are confronted by equally basic differences in social, political, and economic philosophy. These we see currently expressed in differences of opinion as to the adequacy of present Federal programs and the desirability of the changes that have been proposed. This is neither the time nor the place to champion or to attack either of these plans. Persons who are far more competent than I have said much and will inevitably say more. It is pertinent, however, that we not only recognize the problems for which we must plan but also that we recognize some of the currents of thought and the direction in which they flow, for they must inevitably affect the direction of our planning.

Essentially, we are faced with the problem of the role of government in medical care. Contrary to the apparent belief of certain persons, this is not a new problem, even in this country. Nor is it a revolutionary one. For well over a century we have been seeing profound changes in our thinking on this problem and in the degree of acceptance of these changes. A century ago there were few who would defend the concept that government has a role to play in providing doctors for the community or, in other words, medical education. Our medical schools, to the extent that they existed in that era, were privately endowed or were proprietary institutions maintained for the personal profit of the faculty. Many physicians learned medicine only through the tutelage of some elder preceptor under whom they had studied.

By the turn of the century, the people, through their governments, had entered into the picture. Medical practice laws had been enacted to dictate professional standards. Preceptor training had been supplanted by formal schools of medicine, and many states had established tax-supported schools in which to train the physicians that were needed to give medical care to their people. These schools were, to be sure, inferior to the better private schools, yet they were a vast improvement over the proprietary colleges or the preceptor training.

As we pass the middle of the century, however, we find that the proprietary institutions have disappeared and the state schools are on a par with those which are endowed. All of the latter, however, are receiving and to a high degree are dependent on generous governmental grants of one sort or another, and it seems inevitable that these grants will increase rather than diminish. Thus within a mere century we have seen governmental participation in medical education grow from virtually nothing to the point at which today it is fast becoming a dominant force. Whether or not this is desirable is a separate issue. The fact is that it has happened, that it exists, and that all the signs point to an increase. Furthermore, it has progressed steadily through diverse eras of political thought, through changes of Administration whether conservative or progressive. It has been a bit of social evolution that we have come to recognize and to accept, and therefore to take into consideration in our planning.

Medical education, however, has not been the only aspect of medical care in which we have witnessed the growing participation of government. Hospitals were at one time solely under private direction. Gradually, as time has passed, we have seen government more and more assume responsibility in this area. General hospitals under city auspices have competed with private hospitals. In the fields of mental illness, tuberculosis, and acute communicable disease, the nongovernmental hospital has almost disappeared. Nursing homes supported by local or state government are appearing, and private hospitals receive financial assistance from the Federal and state governments under the Hill-Burton funds. To an increasing degree, therefore, government has shared the burden of providing hospital facilities, even to the point of virtual usurpation in certain fields.

It is not alone in medical education and hospitalization that government has been assuming a role of increasing importance in the provision of medical care. The medical care of the indigent, whether on an institutional or a clinic or a home basis, has long been recognized as an ultimate governmental responsibility, even though this burden has often been relieved in part by the invaluable assistance of nonofficial agencies. In recent years we have seen the extension of care to encompass groups not usually considered as truly indigent. One need only mention the Federal and state programs for crippled children as an example of such a development. Current legislation seems certain to add immensely to the number of those who will be so assisted. The provision for free choice of physicians, which is already incorporated into much legislation and is being militantly championed by the advocates and even the opponents of current legislation, is bound to have a profound effect on our medical and hospital programs; for it will inevitably result in channeling patients from the tax-supported to the private hospitals, from the teaching institutions to those that are not suitable for medical education. Thus, more physicians will practice under financial conditions set by government, and the private hospitals will receive a higher proportion of their patients under such regulations. When we recall the extent to which the present hospital population is made up of those who will inevitably be covered by the provisions of such legislation, we can begin to appreciate the impact that this legislation will have upon the distribution of hospital patients and the problems that will confront our medical schools when they attempt to find an adequate supply of suitable patients for clinical teaching.

All of this has its bearing upon our growing problems of health care of the aged. I remarked earlier that we must adjust our thinking and our planning in the direction of control rather than prevention of disease. This will of necessity involve medical care, both in diagnosis and in treatment. We are thus going to be faced more and more with the question of the extent to which government will participate in medical care, recognizing that through a process of social and economic evolution it has, during the past century, already assumed vastly increased responsibility in this field. Furthermore, recognizing that, whether we approve or disapprove, the trend is toward increased participation, we must decide as to what direction this participation will take. I can only hope and pray that we may, through intelligent and constructive planning, evolve a formula which will place government in the role of supplementing rather than supplanting the private physician-patient relationship. This I see as one of the major challenges of present trends, and I hope we may have the foresight to reach solutions which we shall not reject in the cold and disenchanting dawn of future years.

THE STATE HOSPITAL AS A CONSULTANT TO THE COMMUNITY

by Joseph F. Toll

SOCIAL WORK consultation in a state hospital setting is a new dimension for our profession. In the experience which I shall describe, social work skills were deployed within the hospital and the community toward the end of permitting hospitalization for mental illness to be invested with more hope and positive feeling than heretofore.

In 1954, Evansville State Hospital "took down the gate and fence" which surrounded it and for the first time invited community groups to the hospital to see and learn about the various new treatment methods. Judges, welfare workers, ministers, physicians, public health nurses, and other interested citizens listened to reports of psychiatry's modern drugs and approaches. Hospital personnel told of efforts to find the cause and cure for mental illness.

Very soon thereafter, community leaders began to hold the State Hospital totally responsible for the "cure" of released patients. Welfare agencies complained, during the years 1956 to 1958, that "uncured" patients were being discharged because of so-called "miracles." It seemed to some people that the old methods of incarceration of the mentally ill were preferable to the red tape, delay, and doubtful results associated with the "new scientific approach" and its screening, protection of civil rights, and concern for the physical and mental well-being of mental patients.

This state hospital, with a 900-bed capacity, has a patient load of 1,200 and serves fifteen counties—fourteen rural and one urban—in southwest Indiana with a total population of 450,000. The hospital is the only public psychiatric facility in this area. Medical and psychiatric services are limited to what family doctors and general hospitals can offer, and several counties have no qualified physician.

During the past four years, an average of 1,000 applications for admission were received annually; 500 patients were actually admitted for treatment each year. The application interview provides the opportunity for the family of the patient, a professional worker, and the patient himself to consult together on the validity and efficacy of his receiving treatment at a given time in a state mental hospital. The application interview is conducted by a psychiatric social worker and reviewed by the Medical Director. Admissions have been sought for mentally retarded persons, alcoholics facing jail sentences, criminals seeking to evade prison terms, persons with marital problems, and those with problems concerning the aged as well as for persons whose mental condition was amenable to treatment in a psychiatric institution. An arrangement whereby consultation could be offered for a six-year period to applicants for admission enabled the Medical Director to establish a basis for brief treatment of those individuals who had some degree of motivation to accept and profit from treatment. The hospital's limited facilities and funds for a treatment program required an extension of the consultation process in order to screen out more carefully those patients who would not benefit from psychiatry.

Until December, 1957, the largest number of admissions were of patients who had been committed by the courts as insane after three doctors had certified the necessity for such action. In January, 1958, a new law went into effect making possible a ninety-day observation period by court commitment, thus eliminating the insanity hearing and loss of civil rights. As a result, in the fiscal year 1959–60, only 4 percent of all our admitted patients had their civil rights removed by court action prior to their admission.[1] During the two-year period 1958–60, of 1,000 who were admitted, only four patients were certified for regular commitment for more than 180 days under the old law. This has been a potent factor in enabling the hospital staff to motivate patients toward quicker rehabilitative results. The question obviously comes to mind: Have we lessened mental illness in southwest Indiana? Perhaps we have contributed in our small way to a reassessment of its frightening implications.

Community attitudes toward our patients have not changed as quickly as the laws were passed, or as hospital treatment methods adjusted to these laws. Many families still had feelings of stigma because of the mental illness and were unable to accept the state hospital as being right for their patient. The patient, too, in many instances found it difficult to accept the hospital for this same reason. Many groups resisted the hospital's effort to release patients who had completed treatment.

Families found it difficult to realize that the mentally ill person had certain rights and capacities as well as weak-

[1] Temporary commitment for ninety days and one ninety-day extension is permitted.

nesses. We found the same attitudes on the part of some professional persons and groups. During 1958 a series of consultations were held with the different county welfare staffs and later with their directors. County officials had used county welfare agencies to pressure the hospital to remove various persons from their communities when nothing else would make them amenable to community living. The public welfare staffs were not happy with this situation but had no other alternative; the new education they had received from the hospital, coupled with mental health association efforts to "keep the mentally ill out of jail," created much confusion for these same welfare workers.

A Workshop on Joint Efforts of Public Welfare Departments and the Social Service Department of the Evansville State Hospital was held at the hospital on March 18, 1958. The conference concerned itself primarily with problems related to Evansville State Hospital admissions. The conference was attended by more than 90 percent of the staffs of the welfare departments of the rural counties as well as by the social service staff of the hospital. These workers had for some years been asking: "How can we help mentally ill recipients who do not wish to seek treatment, or who enter the hospital without notifying the welfare worker?" The welfare worker would often learn that a person had been admitted to the hospital only after the admission had created an emergency in his home. The psychiatric social worker discovered that in hurried hospital admissions the emotional state of the family often prevented them from giving accurate information about the patient. Sometimes the families would give only negative aspects of the patients' illness and behavior, thus making his treatment and rehabilitation more difficult for the entire staff.

The county welfare worker's long years of experience, knowledge, and observation of the community enable her to make rather accurate judgments as to why persons apply to the state hospital. These workers know their neighbors' aspirations, how long and in what way many of them were being thwarted, or were thwarting themselves. It was more natural for welfare workers to recognize and become related to the social goals which patients and their families were striving toward than it was for them to secure details about pathology. The welfare departments had used the hospital in the past as a place for persons for whom there was no alternative. They quickly recognized that to continue on this basis would be wasteful of hospital facilities and perhaps harmful to the patients. The county welfare staffs and the hospital social workers were ready to plan together for the handling of emergencies.

On April 30, 1958, the welfare directors of eleven rural counties met to consider what services could be provided in emergency cases. Studies of hospital admissions were presented. These studies, made by the hospital social service staff, indicated that on the basis of past patient movement into the hospital, it was unlikely that any one rural county welfare department would be involved in more than twelve emergencies in any one year. In view of such a manageable number of cases, the directors indicated their willingness to cooperate with the hospital to provide some social evaluation material on persons seeking admission. Orientation on the information needed by the medical staff was provided.

From January through March, 1959, the Psychiatric Social Service Administrator visited each of the fourteen rural counties. Consultations were held with the welfare directors, county judges, and court clerks, for the purpose of sharing their experiences with the new Temporary Commitment Law. The judges and county clerks were meeting with resistance to the new law from the families of patients, since in the past commitment had traditionally alluded to insanity trials and hearings. In several counties, judges referred to hearings they had held under this law as "sanity hearings." As these experiences were discussed, the welfare departments indicated that they were ready to help judges and county clerks in implementing the new law, in the event of an emergency. Judges expressed their appreciation for content that could be used in hearings related to the new law. Welfare workers, judges, county clerks, and other county officials were all beginning to interpret to families the use of a temporary commitment as an opportunity to discover the nature of a mental illness.

After several other conferences at the hospital, we published a pamphlet, *Admissions and Releases,* which was made available to all professionals and officials using hospital consultations. In this pamphlet is an outline of various responsibilities that welfare workers help families carry in connection with admission, treatment, and release of patients. The pamphlet has received wide circulation in the fifteen counties.

Forty percent of the most difficult admissions from rural counties were assisted by welfare departments from April, 1959, to April, 1960. The departments used consultation from the hospital in all these cases. The number of hospital consultations concerning aged persons and children increased markedly, and admissions of these cases were substantially reduced. Patients were being prepared for a brief treatment at the hospital, and more attention was given to provision of proper clothing and pocket money for the patient and visiting and writing him during his hospitalization. Sheriffs were spending more time in securing the cooperation of patients who were admitted as "dangerous" cases. A relationship was established between hospital staff, county welfare staffs, and county clerks which practically eliminated calls from the Governor, or other high-ranking officials, because of the state hospital's refusal to take certain patients.

The early efforts of the welfare departments were motivated primarily by a desire to do something to help the hospital in its over-all program. In October, 1959, all fifteen county welfare directors again met at Evansville to review their joint efforts to help the mentally ill. After their two years of cooperation, they expressed concern over when and how they could help families who exerted pressure in an effort to force a commitment so as to relieve themselves of a painful situation. The welfare directors faced directly the question as to whether they were helping the hospital or the person when they handled decisions related to hospital admissions. What should be done when the welfare department felt that it would be helpful to an applicant or to his relative to have the application interview take place at the state hospital? The psychiatric social worker wanted also to relate to what applicants and their families were seeking in a psychiatric hospital experience. It was agreed that welfare departments would only interview families and patients for social histories when the welfare worker felt that this service would help his client to be more planful and would help each person to see the steps he could take when he applied to the state hospital. In some instances, one step might involve an interview at the state hospital. The welfare staffs also felt that they wanted to offer service when treatment was indicated but conditions made a trip to the hospital for an application interview impossible. Hospital and welfare staffs could see their respective parts in helping make application to the hospital a responsible experience.

We then considered the hospital's concern about releases. Many patients remained for long periods of time because their families were either fearful or not interested enough to make release plans with, or for, the patient. The hospital staff, appreciative of the pressures and heavy caseloads of the welfare departments and the service already rendered to the hospital program, hesitated to ask for help with release planning. Several county judges had agreed to call in relatives who refused to get in touch with the hospital about their responsibilities, and the welfare departments were made aware of this fact. It was hoped that such legal approaches would be used only as a last resort, after all voluntary efforts to work together had failed.

Welfare personnel questioned their competence in regard to giving service as part of the release-planning phase of the hospital social service program. From their past experience, it was possible to help the welfare staffs recognize their competence in providing social evaluations as they gave service to applicants for hospitalization. The medical staff of the hospital agreed that this same competence was most valuable to the patients at the point of release planning. With this reassurance from the hospital staff and a two-year working relationship, the group expressed the conviction that there was nothing to stop the welfare departments from trying to help with release planning.[2]

[2] Joseph F. Toll, "These Are Our People," *Public Welfare,* XIX (1961), 23–28

In a similar way, the hospital tackled the more complex task of releasing patients to the community with the support of kindred professional groups and agencies. It was not possible, with the hospital's limited professional staff, to provide after-care follow-up services. However, in October, 1958, the medical staff began to send written reports to family physicians when patients were released. In the spring of 1959, the Southwest Indiana Medical Society was invited to the hospital by the Medical Director because of the many inquiries which general practitioners had made about hospital treatment practices and new laws which concerned mental hospitals. (This meeting supplemented two previous county medical society meetings which were held at the hospital.) Following the meeting, the reports submitted to the family doctors became more meaningful to them, and they in turn became more supportive of the patients' renewed efforts to face the community after hospitalization. From October, 1958, to February, 1960, 195 physicians received reports on 412 patients released from the hospital.

These reports were written by the Medical Superintendent and included a summary of diagnosis and treatment, family plans, and names of interested persons or agencies. An analysis of these reports revealed many interesting facts about discharge rates and characteristics of patients: [3]

1. Eighty-seven percent came into the hospital with their civil rights intact, either voluntarily or by court commitment, or for purpose of observation. Thirteen percent were declared insane in the courts and their civil rights were removed.

[3] Milton H. Anderson, M.D., and Joseph F. Toll, "Current Trends in Public and Private Agency Services to *Patients on After-Care Status*," paper presented at the National Conference on Social Welfare, 1960.

	Percent
2. Diagnosed as having functional disorders	79
Diagnosed as having organic impairment	21
Under 20	5
21 to 64 age group	77
65 years and older	18
3. Released within 3 months of treatment	57
Released within 6 months of treatment	23
Released within 12 months of treatment	15
Total released in one year	95

A cursory check revealed that a large number of patients were going to general medical practitioners and were asking for their help at time of release. Many of these doctors were then calling the hospital for a psychiatric consultation, which they received from the Medical Director and his staff. Another recent development has been that the family doctor often calls the hospital to plan a temporary stay for a patient as part of a treatment plan which was begun in the hospital. The family doctor stands ready to continue with the patient after a second release.

The county welfare departments began to receive requests from family doctors to help with released patients, and these requests in many instances were based on the hospital reports. The chief social worker of the hospital was invited to several rural county medical society meetings to discuss closer collaboration between the general practitioners and the state hospital. At one medical society meeting the psychiatric social worker was confronted with many questions regarding the county welfare department's apparent influence with the state hospital in admitting patients. The doctors, while critical, were primarily concerned about efficient treatment procedures. It became clear, however, that they had not brought their concern for their mentally ill patients to the attention of the hospital as forthrightly as they might have. They cited many aspects of their practice which had helped mentally ill persons. The physicians indicated that they wanted a closer tie with the hospital, and were most appreciative of the hospital's willingness to work with them on a collaborative basis.

In this same county, following this meeting, there were several instances of hospital admission in which the welfare department and the family doctor collaborated and succeeded in eliminating completely the use of insanity hearings by the court. Since January, 1960, court commitments from this county to the state hospital are on an "observation basis," and physicians and the welfare department cooperate in mapping release plans. All cases admitted from this county from January to November, 1960, involved cooperation between the welfare department and a local physician. Prior to admission, many younger patients have been referred for hospital treatment on the short-term basis, whereas formerly there would have been an attempt merely to remove them from the community. Recently, in the case of a fifty-one-year-old chronic former patient, family doctor, relative, state hospital, and nursing home combined efforts to plan for temporary nursing home care. The patient's relative needed a month's vacation to recharge herself so that she could continue the home care of the patient. The family doctor helped plan a "vacation" for the patient in a nursing home and the vacation for the relative, with the state hospital standing by in the event that psychiatric treatment should be required before the relative returned.

In many instances, the Superintendent's individual consultations with physicians regarding aged and child applicants enabled these physicians to use their welfare departments to make other plans. From October, 1958, to October, 1960, the use of the county jail to house mentally ill persons pending their admission to the state hospital ceased in several rural counties. Consultations with physicians and welfare workers in these counties were directly responsible for the establishment of special security rooms in local hospitals to be used by applicants for the brief waiting period before they would enter the state hospital. Physicians began to use ataractic drugs and pay more attention to patients during the waiting period with the result that many patients went home after several weeks. One county physician reported that more than 50 patients were given short-term treatment for mental illness in security rooms in a one-year period; heretofore, this same county averaged twelve admissions a year to the state hospital.

Public health nurses in the urban county began a preventive service on a trial basis (in collaboration with the state hospital) to help emotionally ill persons seek examination from a general physician prior to their application to the state hospital. The hospital implemented orientation to the welfare departments through a series of bulletins that explained what steps the hospital, families, or community resources might take in regard to certain types of cases, such as criminal sexual psychopaths, alcoholics, and the aged.

In October, 1960, when the county welfare directors met at the hospital to consider collaborative efforts to date, a representative of the State Board of Health was present. Hospital staff and welfare personnel reviewed many instances of working together for mental health. Out of this conference came a further attempt by the State Board of

Health to contribute in some part to the public health phase of mental illness.

Having become interested in the extent to which public health services for the mentally ill could be introduced to several rural counties, the State Board of Health discovered the necessity of a consultation program with county health officers. The following report of the meeting with some of these county health officers, on November 9, 1960, was submitted by the State Board of Health physician in charge of special services:

MEETING ON THE CARE OF MENTAL PATIENTS

On November 9, 1960, a meeting for representatives from Evansville State Hospital, from local health departments, and from the Indiana State Board of Health was held to discuss ways and means whereby local health resources could be used to assist persons who may be in need of mental health care and to assist families of mentally ill persons.

It was brought out that Evansville State Hospital will aid physicians who need assistance or information relative to the sending of a patient to the hospital. This can be done by calling the hospital for consultation. It was felt that local health departments would be in a good position of informing the community of this service.

The assistance that a public health nurse might give in the mental health program was discussed. The county health nurse often times has information or is able to secure information which would assist the hospital in the care of patients in the hospital or discharge of patients back to their communities. An example was given where the health department, through its nurse, was instrumental in getting a patient under care before serious consequence resulted. At other times when a patient is discharged from the hospital follow-up is needed to see if a patient is remaining under the care of a physician.

Figures collected by the hospital were presented showing the number of patients admitted from various communities, number discharged to the communities and the number of inquiries from various communities regarding help in obtaining psychiatric care for patients in need of it.

It was decided that in communities where the health officer felt that it was feasible for his department to participate the health officer should be contacted to explore how his department could contribute.

The rural counties are collaborating with the hospital in admissions and planning releases. The hospital and health officers are now ready to strengthen the ties established between the hospital and the community. Judges, physicians, welfare personnel, and nurses are beginning to recognize that the state hospital is only a part, although a significant part, of a total community mental health effort. Various kinds of social and legal problems that relate to the mentally ill are being considered by more professional groups than heretofore. We would like to believe that the state hospital consultation services have contributed in some way toward this development.

A COMMUNITY-WIDE APPROACH TO ADEQUATE SALARIES

by C. B. Olmsted

THE BASIC QUESTION to which the Cleveland job evaluation project [1] addresses itself may be simply stated as follows: How can we make the most productive use of community funds available for salaries in the field of social welfare and health?

Time may prove that seeking answers to this question is the route which leads most directly to more money being made available for salaries. If so, this fact has not yet been demonstrated in Cleveland. There is, however, substantial evidence of a growing conviction about the direct relationship between adequate salaries and the production of efficient and effective services.

In 1956, salaries for professional casework practitioners averaged well below the minimums of the ranges established by the pilot study. For example, salaries for "Caseworker C" positions, beginning positions for which the master's degree is a minimum requirement, averaged $316 per month. This compared with a minimum rate of $385 recommended for this position in 1957. Similarly, the highest level of direct-service (nonsupervisory) casework job—

[1] A job evaluation and salary study of professional, clerical, and maintenance occupation in ninety-six autonomous member organizations of the Cleveland Welfare Federation.

"Caseworker F"—averaged $477 in 1956, compared to a recommended minimum of $564 per month in 1957.

Between 1957 and 1960 the salary range guides based on the pilot study were raised twice to reflect increases in community rates for comparable jobs. For 1959, the annual survey of business rates for jobs comparable to casework positions indicated an upward adjustment in the ranges of 5 percent. For 1960 the ranges were again increased, by 3 percent.

During this period, 1956–60, casework agencies supported by the Cleveland Community Chest received 19 percent *additional* funds for salaries. Salaries for the casework jobs included in the study, however, were increased by an average of 35 percent. Rates for "Caseworker C" and "Caseworker F" moved, by even greater percentages than this average, to $432 and $684 respectively during the four-year interval ending in 1960. (It should be borne in mind that these rates are for nonsupervisory positions.)

A small proportion of the money for these increases, over and above new allocations received, has come to hand through raising fees for service and through reducing nonpersonnel costs. Most of it, however, is the direct result of effort by management to increase the efficiency of personnel. By this I mean that the same or even greater productivity is being achieved by fewer people, or through more extensive use of personnel in lower and less costly classifications.

Agency executives and board members tend to point to a common reason for their willingness to experiment with fairly drastic efficiency measures. The reason is that they are convinced of the fairness of, and necessity for, paying within the ranges recommended by the study at all the levels of knowledge and skill required to fulfill the functions of their respective organizations. In my opinion, it is often easier to convince boards and budget committees than agency executives that 1961 ranges such as the following are *conservative* for jobs with responsibilities as described in Volume II of the project report: [2]

Salary Grade VI: Senior teacher, nursery and/or special fields, $5,544–7,488
Salary Grade VIII: Group worker C, $6,708–9,396
Salary Grade X: Casework supervisor, D, $8,124–11,784

By January, 1960, Arthur H. Kruse, General Secretary of the Cleveland Family Service Association, was able to report for his agency that:

> Out of 55 professional persons on the staff, 27 are now earning better than $8,000 a year and of this number 16 are earning better than $9,000. Incidentally, professional staff turnover for the past two years has averaged 10 percent a year compared with an average turnover of 20 percent over the previous six years.[3]

Smaller agencies have found it more difficult to produce substantial savings by reducing personnel. Nevertheless, since the start of the community-wide job classification and salary guide study in 1959, salaries for all jobs in all Chest-supported agencies have been increased by substantially more than additional funds alone would have accomplished. This has happened despite a marked drop in the percentages of over-all increases in the Chest campaign results during the past three years. Table 1 illustrates the difference in agency applications of funds to increase salaries:

[2] *Jobs and Salaries in Health and Welfare,* 2 vols. (Cleveland: Cleveland Welfare Federation, 1960).

[3] Arthur H. Kruse, "A 1960 Appraisal of Graduates of Professional Education as Observed in Practice," paper presented at the Annual Meeting of the Council on Social Work Education, Oklahoma City, January 23, 1960.

TABLE 1

Year	*Percent Increase in Allocation to Agencies for All Salaries*	*Percent by Which Agencies Increased All Salaries*
1955	2.7	3.4
1956	6.2	6.6
1957	8.4	9.1
1958	5.0	5.4
1959 (start of project)	1.0	2.4
1960 (completion of project)	3.0	5.4
1961	2.0	3.1

To summarize: During the four years prior to the community wide job study, Cleveland's sixty Chest agencies increased salaries by an average of 9 percent more than the additional funds allocated to them for salary increases. From 1959, when all but one of these agencies commenced participation in the study, to the present year they have increased salaries by 80 percent more than the additional funds allocated to them for salary increases.

Job evaluation is not new to our field. We have forms of it in most of our tax-supported programs around the country. It has been applied in some manner in a number of major cities. In some cases it has led to central control of salary administration, which has of course made it unpopular with organizations which derive their major strength from their autonomy. The Cleveland application has from the start attempted to avoid implications of central control. As one of the personnel specialists from the business field who has acted as a volunteer leader in this effort for several years puts it:

In the typical social agency the executive is his own personnel administrator. Personnel men from business may be able to help him by making available for his use: (1) tested personnel methods, and (2) current and factual community-wide information about personnel practices and salaries. Only the executive and his board, however, can decide what part of this information is applicable in his organization and how it shall be applied.

The use of the business field's job evaluation method provides the most thorough means I know of for developing conviction among business leaders about the need for more adequate salaries in social health and welfare programs. Top executives participated in the decisions to undertake and finance the project. Their personnel directors designed the study approach to the satisfaction both of agency administration and of business management. Then these volunteers guided every phase of the study along lines widely accepted at all management levels of business since the Second World War. Their confidence was first evidenced in their sponsorship of requests for $45,000 to underwrite the costs. This budget was met jointly by the Cleveland Foundation, the Morris and Bertha Treuhaft Memorial Fund of the Jewish Community Federation, and the Welfare Federation itself from its reserve funds.

Of course, some of the most extensive and creative business leadership and involvement came in the development of job comparisons between their own field and the field under study. It was business personnel leadership which, as early as 1954, questioned the traditional comparison of social work salaries with those of teachers, nurses, and librarians and thus led to the pioneering look toward industry taken by the pilot project. "How can we hope," they asked, "to solve our problems of personnel shortages and high turnover if we use as our basic reference points in salary administration only fields which are characterized by the same problems?"

In January, 1960, a set of thirteen summaries of technical and professional jobs commonly found in health and welfare agencies was under independent study in 125 Cleveland businesses. We did our best to include in the survey all types of business firms represented in the economy. Fifty-six of these firms found at least one health or welfare job which, in their judgment, compared with a job in their own organization. Some found as many as ten of the thirteen jobs which they could compare to jobs in their respective companies—companies, for the most part, which employ several hundred or a thousand persons. Since these comparisons are listed in the study report, I shall not detail them here.

In addition to all pertinent salary information, each participating company submitted a written description of each job considered comparable to one covered by the study. This made it possible for the Evaluation Committee to review and pass on all business jobs which were eventually included for salary comparison purposes. Following the traditions established by the pilot study, the committee acted conservatively. The comparisons proposed by business which were discarded by the committee, as too far removed from service to people, would have increased the disparity which the project revealed between salaries in the two fields.

The 1960 project produced four separate salary structures for executive and administrative jobs; technical and professional jobs; clerical jobs; and maintenance jobs. Executive classifications and salary ranges have been treated as confidential, the executive and board president of each agency receiving only the information pertinent to his agency. Guides for all four categories were established by essentially the same procedures, and all of the plans except the executive guides are shown and explained in Volume I of the published report.

Agency salaries.—In January, 1960, after the evaluation of technical and professional jobs was completed, each participating agency was asked to report its present salaries for all positions. Table 2 cites some examples of the rates reported:

TABLE 2

Salary Grade	*Job Title*	*Evaluation Point Rating*	*Range of Monthly Rates*	*Average*
I	Nurses aide [a]	488	$130–228	$178
II	Junior teacher, nursery and/or special fields	541	215–340	277
III	Child care worker	595	150–375	249
IV	Nurse, institutional [a]	648	220–370	312
V	Caseworker C	724	300–500	432
VI	Senior teacher, nursery and/or special fields	761	308–433	375
VII	Caseworker D	807	358–685	494
VIII	Group worker C	883	408–775	537
IX	Caseworker F	928	525–770	684
X	Casework supervisor D	940	534–783	713

[a] Nonhospital

Average rates for the casework jobs shown are relatively high for their evaluation ratings. This result might be expected, since salaries for these jobs have been the focus of attention since the 1956 pilot study. In general, this picture could only arouse concern about present rates for technical and professional jobs in Cleveland agencies. When both evaluation points and salaries for typical jobs in this category are averaged, the composite job is one of about the complexity of the beginning social work job requiring full professional training (master's degree) with an average salary of $400 per month, or $4,800 per year.

Comparable business rates.—At the same time, the area survey of rates for comparable business jobs showed an average salary for comparable positions of approximately $605 per month, or $7,260 per year. In other words, business rates averaged about 50 percent higher than agency salaries for comparable jobs.

The salary range guides.—Salary administration specialists recommend a variety of approaches that will enable us to work from these current agency salaries, and the discrepancies with going rates for comparable jobs in the community, toward a unified salary structure. The best of these approaches, in my opinion, rely heavily on the good judgment of persons informed about management objectives and conditions in the social work field. In this case, all the available data were studied carefully by several groups of volunteer personnel experts from Cleveland businesses, most of whom were by this time thoroughly familiar with jobs and salaries in the participating agencies.

The first step was to separate the evaluated jobs into salary grades. After experimenting with a variety of divisions, it was concluded that a consistent progression of fifty job difficulty points would provide groupings which reflect with greatest justice the evaluation results for each job.

Several approaches to the determination of minimum and maximum rates for each classification were also considered. In the last analysis, it was decided that the data implied a holding over for 1961 of the ranges recommended for casework jobs in 1960 through the updating process of the pilot study which has been described. This conclusion, conservative though it was, still meant that many rates for jobs newly incorporated into the project would fall well below the minimums of the ranges recommended for 1961. It placed the maximums of the ranges at about the average rates paid in Cleveland business for comparable jobs.

Every point in this salary structure is now related mathematically to every other point in the following way:

1. As we have already seen, each of the ten salary grades encompasses fifty job difficulty points.

2. The minimum of each grade is 10 percent above the minimum of the preceding grade, providing for a wide overlapping of the ranges. The spread between the minimum and maximum of the first three grades is 30 percent. As job complexity increases, this spread increases to 35 percent for grades IV, V, and VI; to 40 percent for grades VII, VIII, and IX; and to 45 percent from the minimum to the maximum of the range for Grade X.

Ranges recommended for 1962.—In March, 1961, the Board of Trustees of the Welfare Federation approved an increase of approximately 4 percent in these ranges for 1962. This action was based upon the results of the annual repetition of the area salary survey, which showed an advance of 4.5 percent in average rates for comparable business jobs covered. Therefore, these salary range guides for 1962 have been adjusted upward without disturbing the basic pattern established for the salary structure. Table 3 shows the annual salaries recommended for 1962 for the ten classifications of technical and professional jobs.

This job classification and salary guide project has resulted in widespread community agreement about what currently constitutes adequate salaries for jobs in health and welfare organizations. The process by which it was carried out, and is kept up to date, has underscored this agreement with conviction about paying these rates. Management groups feel an obligation to the community to pay them. Community leaders believe that this is necessary to assure the continuing possibility of staffing jobs required to fulfill necessary community functions with personnel who have the required knowledge, skill, and imagination.

TABLE 3

Salary Grade	*Job Title*	*Annual Range Recommended for 1962*
I	Nurses aide [a]	$3,564– 4,632
II	Junior teacher, nursery and/or special fields	3,924– 5,100
III	Child care worker	4,320– 5,616
IV	Nurse, institutional [a]	4,752– 6,420
V	Caseworker C	5,232– 7,068
VI	Senior teacher, nursery and/or special fields	5,760– 7,776
VII	Caseworker D	6,336– 8,868
VIII	Group worker C	6,972– 9,756
IX	Caseworker F	7,668–10,740
X	Casework supervisor D	8,436–12,228

[a] Nonhospital

In attempting to implement this community-wide agreement and conviction, new questions arise and old ones are raised again with new urgency:

Are existing standards of productivity for professional jobs, and present systems of performance appraisal, adequate to assure agency management that it is getting its money's worth out of a $7,000, $9,000, or $11,000 position?

How can the efficiency of operation of an agency be

judged fairly? A committee which budgets several agencies, voluntary or tax supported, may have a total of 3 percent additional money for salaries. Agency requests may range from 4 percent to 14 percent, with each claiming that its request is the minimum needed to implement the study guides. The "have" agencies, needing about 4 percent, argue that the available money should be allocated 3 percent across the board. The "have nots," who need up to 14 percent, call for a differential approach to allocations to enable them to close the gap. How can the budget committee know that by giving a disproportionate amount to those that are behind it is not penalizing the ones ahead for having been efficient?

Long-familiar problems of administration still recur when additional funds for salaries are severely limited, as they were during the last three years in Cleveland. Then, the pressure, implied by relatively high salary standards, to increase efficiency tends to wear thin the patience of conscientious agency workers and executives. They remind the community that: (1) in fairness, it must be as much concerned with agency efficiency in fat years as in lean; (2) calling for more efficiency is not an acceptable substitute for raising the additional funds needed to finance the desired levels of agency services; and (3) effective service to people is not rendered by the numbers—quantity alone cannot measure the professional job.

Despite the persistence of such problems, members of the staffs, administrations, boards, and budget committees, together with other business and community leaders in Cleveland, have found the job study a focal point in their joint effort to achieve and maintain adequate salaries in the field of health and welfare.

A developing community philosophy of salary administration, based on systematic job evaluation and tied to current business rates, gives grounds for optimism that money will continue to follow intentions.

Papers presented at the 88th Annual Forum may also be found in *The Social Welfare Forum, 1961* (published by Columbia University Press); and in *Casework Papers, 1961* and *New Perspectives on Group Work: Theory, Organization, and Practice,* information concerning which may be obtained from the National Conference on Social Welfare.